*Living the Catechism of the Catholic Church*

CHRISTOPH SCHÖNBORN, O.P.

# Living the

# Catechism of the Catholic Church

*A Brief Commentary on the Catechism
for Every Week of the Year*

VOLUME THREE

LIFE IN CHRIST

TRANSLATED BY MICHAEL J. MILLER

IGNATIUS PRESS    SAN FRANCISCO

Title of the German original:
*Wähle das Leben*
*Die christliche Moral nach dem Katechismus der Katholischen Kirche*
© 1998 Dom-Verlag, Vienna

English translation of the *Catechism of the Catholic Church* for the
United States of America copyright © 1994, United States
Catholic Conference, Inc.—Libreria Editrice Vaticana.
English translation of the *Catechism of the Catholic Church:
Modifications from the Editio Typica* copyright © 1997,
United States Catholic Conference, Inc.—Libreria Editrice
Vaticana. Used with permission.

Cover design by Riz Boncan Marsella

© 2001 Ignatius Press, San Francisco
ISBN 0–89870–835–4
Library of Congress control number 95–75670
Printed in the United States of America ∞

Dedicated to
the religion teachers
of our Archdiocese
as a sign of appreciation,
thanks, and encouragement.

# Contents

|  | Foreword | 9 |
| 1. | Christian, recognize your dignity! | 11 |
| 2. | The foundation | 13 |
| 3. | The goal | 16 |
| 4. | Freedom | 19 |
| 5. | Acting humanly | 22 |
| 6. | The passions | 25 |
| 7. | Conscience | 28 |
| 8. | Virtue | 31 |
| 9. | Prudence | 33 |
| 10. | Justice | 35 |
| 11. | Fortitude | 38 |
| 12. | Temperance | 40 |
| 13. | Natural and supernatural virtues | 43 |
| 14. | Faith | 46 |
| 15. | Hope | 49 |
| 16. | Charity | 52 |
| 17. | The gifts of the Holy Spirit | 55 |
| 18. | What is sin? | 58 |
| 19. | Grave sin—light sin | 61 |
| 20. | Community | 64 |
| 21. | Authority | 67 |
| 22. | The common good | 69 |
| 23. | Equality and diversity | 71 |
| 24. | The law | 73 |
| 25. | Grace | 76 |

| 26. | Merit | 79 |
| 27. | Called to holiness | 82 |
| 28. | Magisterium and morality | 85 |
| 29. | The Ten Commandments | 88 |
| 30. | You shall believe in one God | 91 |
| 31. | Religion is not a private matter | 93 |
| 32. | You shall not make for yourself an image | 96 |
| 33. | God's Name is holy | 99 |
| 34. | You shall keep holy the Lord's day | 102 |
| 35. | Honor your father and your mother | 105 |
| 36. | The family | 108 |
| 37. | Superiors | 110 |
| 38. | Church and state | 113 |
| 39. | You shall not kill! | 116 |
| 40. | Defending life—comprehensively | 118 |
| 41. | Death penalty? | 121 |
| 42. | War and peace | 124 |
| 43. | The sixth commandment | 127 |
| 44. | Open to life | 130 |
| 45. | The seventh commandment | 133 |
| 46. | Theft | 135 |
| 47. | Responsibility for creation | 138 |
| 48. | Truthfulness | 141 |
| 49. | Media ethics | 144 |
| 50. | Art, the true and the beautiful | 147 |
| 51. | You shall not covet | 149 |
| 52. | The spirit's yearning | 151 |
| | Abbreviations | 155 |

# Foreword

"Teacher, what good deed must I do, to have eternal life?" To this question of the rich young man, Jesus gives a clear, concise answer: "If you would enter life, keep the commandments" (Mt 19:16–17).

The question of what is good moves every human being, even the one who represses it. Anyone who does not ask it anymore, who is no longer concerned about it at all, becomes "inhuman". The question of what is good, together with the search for what is true, has been part of being human from the very beginning until today. The question about "eternal life", which the rich young man poses to Jesus, has likewise moved humanity since its earliest beginnings. What happens after death? And what should *this* life be like so as not to forfeit *eternal* life? Today, this question no longer seems to disturb many people. It appears as if many view earthly life as "all there is". A quick glance over the history of mankind reveals, on the contrary, that these two questions were always connected—the question about what is good and the one about eternal life. Only a *good* life leads to *eternal* life: all religions know about this correlation. Furthermore, all of them know to some extent that neither of these is achieved without toil and danger, that we need help from above in order to do good and avoid evil. The rich young man suspects this, too. Therefore he turns to a teacher: "What must I do . . . ?" From the Teacher he hopes to obtain direction and assistance.

Since those days when the voice of the Teacher resounded, when he showed us the way of life, countless numbers have put his teaching to the test and experienced that he, Jesus Christ, really is "the way, and the truth, and the life" (Jn 14:6). "Christian morality" is not an abstract collection of rules, but rather entrance into a relationship with him, the imitation of Christ. The great models and examples of morality, therefore, are the saints, those people in whose lives the way of Jesus shines and is made concrete in a special way. There is no clearer testimony to the humanity and the beauty of Christian morality than the lives of the saints. That these examples are not distant and unattainable, that holiness is open to all as a way and a goal, is one of the great themes of the Second Vatican Council. May the following fifty-two chapters be read as an encouragement to follow the Teacher more and more, utterly and entirely, so that we "may have life, and have it abundantly" (Jn 10:10).

+ Christoph Schönborn
Archbishop of Vienna

Feast of Saint Augustine
August 28, 1998

# Christian, recognize your dignity!

For the third time now I am beginning a series of brief commentaries on the *Catechism of the Catholic Church*, eight million copies of which have already been printed in various editions worldwide (the most recent translations published are the Chinese and the Russian). In many parts of the world the *Catechism* is already completely integrated into the life of the Church and now constitutes an indispensable tool in the work of catechesis, for preaching, for group study, and for personal meditation. Even though this process is taking place more slowly in our area [in Austria], it still cannot be overlooked. May the fifty-two short *Catechism* meditations that follow offer some small encouragement to reach more often and more confidently for the *Catechism*!

The third part of the *Catechism*, which is the subject of this new series, deals with Christian morality. Today public opinion usually associates this term with things that are outmoded, antiquated, narrow, out-of-touch, and counterproductive. It is especially associated with prohibitions, in particular, those falling under the sixth commandment. People who leave the Church often give as their reason that it is impossible (or no longer possible) for them to deal with the Christian notions of morality. Especially among young people one often runs up against a complete lack of appreciation for Christian morality, or, more precisely, for what they imagine that term to mean.

Is Christian morality, though, what it is understood to be in the mass media and public opinion? What is it really like, this "rule of life" that Christ gave to his disciples and which we are invited to live by? Many parents today ask themselves this question when they try to recommend to their children a life lived according to the faith. For all those who proclaim the faith, the urgent question arises again and again: What does a faith-filled, Christian life look like today?

To all these questions the *Catechism* gives only an indirect answer. Its specific purpose is to present the teachings of the Christian faith organically (CCC 18) and thus to help deepen the understanding of faith (CCC 23). Included in this is a more accurate knowledge of what Christian morality teaches, which is often misunderstood and rejected simply out of ignorance. A better understanding, a deeper knowledge, though, can also help a person say Yes to the Christian way of life and to appreciate it better.

Yet before we embark on our consideration of this way of life, a fundamental observation is necessary: Christian morality is not discovered primarily through knowledge and reason, as important as these are, but rather through the concrete following of Christ. Someone who sets out upon the "way of Christ" (CCC 1696), who tries with the help of grace to live a life "'worthy of the gospel of Christ'" (Phil 1:27, quoted in CCC 1692), will also discover the meaning of God's commandments in an entirely new way; for him they will prove to be pathways to life, to a happy life.

# *The foundation*

" 'Christian, recognize your dignity . . .' " (St. Leo the Great, *Sermo 21 in nat. Dom.*, 3: PL 54, 192C, quoted in CCC 1691). With this saying of Pope Saint Leo the Great (440–461) the *Catechism* begins its third part, on Christian morality, which can be summarized in one sentence, which likewise comes from Pope Leo: Do not live beneath your dignity.

Human dignity—this keyword recurs in contemporary discussions of morality, ethics, and moral philosophy like a leitmotiv. Human rights depend entirely and absolutely upon an appreciation of human dignity. In what, though, does the dignity of man consist, in particular, the dignity of the Christian?

The answer to this question, in turn, depends on one's image of man. The answer to the question "Who is man?" largely determines one's view of human dignity and also of what constitutes ethics or morality. The question of the image of man is therefore the question of the foundation of morality.

"But what is man? He has put forward, and continues to put forward, many views about himself, views that are divergent and even contradictory. Often he either sets himself up as the absolute measure of all things, or debases himself to the point of despair." Thus says the Council in its great document about morality, in the Pastoral Constitution on the Church in the Modern

World (*GS* 12). It makes a great difference whether man is viewed in a purely materialistic way, as a mere product of evolution, of the material processes of the cosmos; whether he is viewed esoterically, in the Gnostic sense that is widespread today, as a "part of God", a "divine Self"; or whether, in the sense found in the Bible, in revelation, he is valued as God's creature, indeed, as " 'the only creature on earth that God has willed for its own sake' " (*GS* 24 § 3, quoted in CCC 1703).

But how do we know what man really is, whether he is a demigod or merely a piece of matter? We believe that, on the one hand, human reason can discover a certain answer. Yet the light of reason is not sufficient. Only the light of revelation gives a solid answer. It knows about man because it sees man as part of God's plan.

The fundamental statement about man stands on the first page of the Bible: "Let us make man in our image, after our likeness" (Gen 1:26). This word is of enormous consequence. Here is the foundation of human dignity. In the image of God—what does that mean?

First of all, that every man possesses a unique, indestructible dignity: he is willed by God, " 'able to know and love his creator' " (*GS* 12 § 3, quoted in CCC 356; see CCC 1700) and hence "capable of understanding the order of things established by the Creator" (CCC 1704). One outstanding manifestation of the divine image in man is his free will (CCC 1705). The image of God also means, however, that man does not have all these things (reason, will, freedom) of his own accord, that he is not completely autonomous and is not a law unto himself. His complete dependence upon the Creator is not a lack of freedom but, rather, the way in which man is free. We receive everything from God: our freedom, our abilities—ultimately, our very selves.

Another part of being in God's image, though, is the fact that—just as God is not alone but rather is a unity of three Divine Persons—so too man is not alone but rather was created as man and woman, as a being capable of communion (CCC 1702).

The foundation of the Christian image of man includes, finally, the knowledge of the drama of sin, of evil, "'at the very beginning of history'" (*GS* 13 § 1, quoted in CCC 1707). The path man walks, therefore, is a life-long battle to avoid evil and to do good. The battle for a life with human dignity is therefore a major theme of Christian teaching about life.

# 3

# The goal

An advertisement for an automobile says: "The way is the goal." But that cannot be right. Someone who is en route without a goal does not have a way and is just wandering around bewildered. We speak of a way only when there is a given orientation, a direction, and thus a goal.

What is the goal of mankind's way? This question is just as important as the one about the foundation of man. The goal determines the way; the way is selected with a view to the goal, in order to reach it as soon and as safely as possible.

But is there a goal that is common to all men? Does not each man, rather, have his own goal that he sets for himself and strives to reach? There is a goal that is common to all men: We all want to be happy! "And not only I myself or a few besides me, but all, we all want to be happy", says Saint Augustine in his *Confessions* (10, 21). A person can seek happiness in many things, along many paths, but no one will sensibly deny that the search for happiness is common to all.

For a long time, too, "morality" was therefore understood as the doctrine of true happiness, as a way to being happy in life (on earth and in eternity). The "natural desire for happiness" is innate; God himself "has placed it in the human heart" (CCC 1718), for "God [is] infinitely perfect and blessed in himself" and wants men, whom he has created in his own image, to "share in his own blessed life" (CCC 1). Therefore God's commandments are not there to spoil our enjoyment of life as men but, rather, to show us the way to a happy life.

Now there is a serious objection to this view of morality as the doctrine of living happily. Is it not our experience that we must do many things that are quite opposed to our pursuit of happiness? Familial, marital, and professional duties often have little regard for our personal wishes. Children are often enticed by something precisely because it is forbidden, and adults, too, know the temptation of "forbidden fruit". And even when we do what is good, is there not a danger of doing it because we enjoy it and not because we really want to help others?

Is the pursuit of happiness not a grand sort of egotism? Should we not do good for its own sake, because it is good, and not because it makes us happy? The dispute among moral philosophers over this question continues to this day.

Life itself teaches us the answer: Not everything we like necessarily leads to happiness (just look at any immoderate behavior!), and not everything we may dislike at the moment leads to unhappiness.

Jesus' Sermon on the Mount is the great guidebook to living happily. The eight Beatitudes (Mt 5:3–12) address ways that make man "blessed", bring him a happiness that is more than being cheerful. Situations and attitudes that from a worldly perspective seem to constitute unhappiness are declared by Jesus to be pathways to happiness: being poor in spirit, mourning, hungering and thirsting for righteousness, being meek and making peace, indeed, being persecuted for righteousness' sake, being slandered for Jesus' sake—all this, Jesus promises, brings blessedness (CCC 1716).

The happiness for which all are striving has received a name and a face: Jesus Christ, the Son of God, "'the image of the invisible God'" (Col 1:15, quoted in CCC 1701; cf. 2 Cor 4:4). He "'makes man fully manifest to man himself and brings to light his exalted vocation'" (*GS* 22 § 1, quoted in CCC 1710). The life experience of so many Christians, saints both known and unknown, testifies that a life led according to the Sermon on the Mount means even now—in the midst of many sorrows and sufferings—incomparable happiness, an anticipation of eternal joy (CCC 1723).

# 4

# *Freedom*

How precious, how wonderful, freedom is often becomes evident only when it is lost. I will never forget meeting with a family of Vietnamese refugees. As "boat people", they had left their land, exposed themselves to serious dangers: pirates and storms, coast guards, thirst and hunger—all this they had taken upon themselves for the sake of one good: in order to attain freedom!

Being made in the image of God, man's chief characteristic is freedom. His freedom reflects the freedom of God (CCC 1730). But what is freedom? The *Catechism* defines it: "Freedom is the power, rooted in reason and will, to act or not to act, to do this or that, and so to perform deliberate actions on one's own responsibility" (CCC 1731).

Where this power is absent or is present only in a limited way, there is no moral responsibility either. The little child and the mentally handicapped person are not held accountable because they cannot responsibly determine their own actions (CCC 1734). External and internal circumstances can diminish freedom (for instance, duress and fear, social pressure or ignorance). Accordingly, imputability is also diminished (CCC 1735).

But what does freedom itself consist of? In this regard there are two deep-seated misunderstandings that must be cleared away. First: we often believe that the more possibilities we have to choose from, the freer we are.

The fatter the catalogue of tours and cruises (and the respective wallet), the freer the customer!

At first it appears that a greater selection adds to freedom. In fact, it is otherwise: I realize my freedom in the measure that I choose the right thing, what is good both for me and in itself. The young person who gives up an "awesome vacation trip" and instead participates in a summer camp for handicapped youngsters only seems to have limited his freedom; in reality he has "actualized", realized, it by voluntarily deciding on something good and committing himself to it. Freedom grows through the deliberate choice of the good; the commitment to it allows freedom to develop (CCC 1733).

The profound misunderstanding of the modern age is believing that human freedom consists in the completely unrestrained, unconditional determination of self, which is limited only from outside, by laws and norms (CCC 1740). In reality it is exactly the reverse: The more we do what is good and practice virtues—this subject will be discussed later—the more firmly established we become in our freedom. For every one of us knows that the dangers to freedom come not only from outside, but even more from ourselves. How easily we misuse it by making it a pretext for convenience, lack of charity, selfishness.

Here we find the second misunderstanding: we are indeed free to choose between good and evil, but our choice of the good or the evil is not without consequences for freedom. The alcoholic is not really free to choose; the addiction draws him to something that he recognizes as harmful. If he manages to get away from alcohol, that is a genuine liberation. It does not mean that in the future he can choose "freely" between drinking and not drinking but, rather, that he has entirely escaped drinking: he has become free through a stable commitment to what is good for him.

We all have to fight the good fight for true freedom. We experience in ourselves also the inclination to evil: "For I do not do the good I want, but the evil I do not want is what I do" (Rom 7:19). Therefore we need to be made free, all of us without exception. " 'For freedom Christ has set us free' " (Gal 5:1, quoted in CCC 1741). The path of imitating Christ is therefore the way of true liberation (CCC 1742). Only when we shall have finally committed our entire being—our understanding and will and all our powers—to God and to our neighbor in charity will we be truly free.

# 5

# Acting humanly

Not everything that we do deserves to be called "human". We spontaneously call a certain action "inhuman", for instance, atrocities, injustices, acts of unkindness. We have a certain "preconceived idea" of what we consider to be "human" or "inhuman". In order to judge whether our action is morally right (good) or morally wrong (evil), therefore, it is important to ask whether it is human, that is, whether it befits us as human beings or whether it debases, injures, or even destroys our humanity. But how do we know what is "human"?

Before we pursue this question (cf. CCC 1749), we must point out another distinction: Not everything we do is necessarily a "human" act. There are actions that are neither good nor evil, because they are not at all subject to our will and thus are not within our power, for instance, all vegetative processes in man, such as the heartbeat or digestion, or nondeliberate behavior like fear and panic. "We can't help it", we say, and we are right. We can voluntarily influence these involuntary processes only to a certain degree—we can become responsible for heart disease through a culpably unhealthy life-style, yet the heart is not at the will's command but is rather spontaneous, acting automatically.

Saint Thomas Aquinas distinguishes, therefore, "acts of man" from "human acts". Only the latter can be evaluated morally, that is, are good or evil, because they are freely and deliberately placed by us, because they are willed (cf. CCC 1749). The former are involuntary. We do not say: My digestion is evil, but rather: It is functioning badly.

In what, then, does the moral quality of a human act consist? How does it become "human"? Christian "moral teaching" distinguishes three elements: the "object" of my action; the end in view or the intention in what I am doing; and the circumstances of this deed (CCC 1750).

Today many people feel that the intention is the decisive thing, and there is some truth to that: A good intention is decisive for the moral quality. A person who prays "in order to be seen by men" perverts something that is good in itself, praying; he misuses something good (CCC 1755). Nevertheless, the first thing to consider is not the intention but, rather, the "object" of the action itself: Praying is "in itself" a good thing; murder is "in itself" an evil thing. How do we know whether something is "in itself" good or evil? Reason and conscience tell us (CCC 1751), if we hear their voice. The Ten Commandments name for us human acts that are always "inhuman", which therefore cannot become good even through a good intention or through special circumstances: denying or blaspheming God, murder, stealing, adultery, or lying. Neither is any of this good when it is done in order to achieve something good ("The end does not justify the means") or when it occurs under great external pressure. Certainly, such pressure (for instance, need, but also societal pressure resulting from the spirit of the age) diminishes responsibility, but it does not make the action right (CCC 1754).

What, then, makes us "human" when we act? A "pure heart", that is, a good will ("blessed are the pure in heart"). We are impressed when we meet upright men. This human rectitude consists of doing what is good and right with an upright heart. To be candid, we know all too well how often the "worm" of vain intentions lies concealed in our good deeds and disturbs or destroys them (CCC 1752). Therefore the way to life is always a struggle to maintain a pure heart.

# 6

# *The passions*

What do passions have to do with morality? Are they not, rather, the opposite of morality? Or at least an obstacle to it? Do we not have to fight against them in order to become respectable, decent human beings? This understanding of the passions is indeed widespread, not only in the common view of what constitutes morality, but also among teachers of philosophy and theology.

It is all the more surprising that the teachers of the medieval period (which is continually misrepresented as a "dark" age) thought quite differently on this subject. Saint Thomas Aquinas explicitly teaches that there can be no "dispassionate" morality. A good life also includes a good measure of passion, though, of course, a restrained passion.

We should explain, then, what is to be understood by "the passions". They are "natural components of the human psyche; they form the passageway and ensure the connection between the life of the senses and the life of the mind" (CCC 1764). The life of our souls consists not only in the exercise of reason and will; we are composed also of "powers of the soul" that extend into the vital realm of sensuality. The Bible speaks of the heart, but also of the bowels (Hebrew *rahamim*, Latin *viscera*), as the seat of these powers.

Two fundamental passions are distinguished in the

ancient and medieval teaching about man: The *concupiscible* power is the yearning, the "passionate" striving for what one recognizes or imagines to be good; the *irascible* power is the angry urge that passionately wards off what it regards as evil, harmful, or something to be avoided.

And now from this we draw a conclusion that surprises many people: There is no human morality without an abundant measure of passion—well-ordered passion, to be sure. Yes, the greater part of moral education, of working to attain moral maturity, consists of forming the passions correctly, of orienting, developing, and applying them. All too well do we know how much havoc, how much evil, the unbridled, disordered passions can cause. Only someone who applies all the powers of his soul for the good can be considered a morally mature man.

This is made most clear in the lives of the saints. Can anyone imagine a Saint Teresa of Avila without a great "irascible" power, completely integrated into her mission, of course, without that vital energy which can withstand adversity, that carries out the responsibilities of a mission with courage and fortitude? She could never have founded so many monasteries if, instead of controlling her irascible power, she had allowed it to dissipate in anger, impatience, sadness. Persevering in a good intention, patience in calamity, spiritual strength in the trials of life—these are indications that the soul's irascible powers have been put entirely in the service of the good.

It is no different with the "concupiscible power"; after all, we are supposed to love God not only with our whole mind and will, but also with all the strength and powers of our soul. The "little way" of Saint Thérèse, the Little Flower, is a school that teaches us to bring all of our wishes and all, even the slightest stirrings of our heart, of our passions, of our longing and yearning, into a love for God and for our neighbor and to direct them to that end. The saints are passionate people; "body and soul", with their whole heart, they are on their way to the good (CCC 1770).

# 7

## Conscience

"He followed his conscience"—that is the title of the biography of the Austrian farmer Franz Jägerstätter, who for religious reasons refused to serve in the military and on that account was put to death by the Nazis. "You should always follow your conscience", we say, and that is right. But is the conscience always right? It can be mistaken, too. Should you still follow it even then? Before a secular court of law it is obviously not enough simply to appeal to one's conscience in order to be acquitted. Is conscience the highest moral court of appeal? Is it, so to speak, the supreme judge?

What is conscience? Let us try to approach this reality by considering its absence. We say that a man "has no conscience" if, for instance, he exploits his subordinates and those who depend on him. We wonder: Doesn't this man's conscience bother him at all? We feel that it is a serious loss of humanity when seemingly or actually a man no longer reacts to his own inhuman behavior with "pangs of conscience".

Conscience is obviously a sort of "court of justice", an internal organ from which we expect approval or rejection, a positive or negative judgment on human attitudes and actions (CCC 1778). The absence of this organ, unscrupulousness or irresponsibility, is a serious deficiency. We also feel, though, that it is intolerable when someone commits deeds of obvious inhumanity under the pretext of following his conscience. Someone who tortures others "with a good conscience" is acting, as we spontaneously judge, either with an unsound mind (insanely) or else as a "moral monster".

This example makes clear something that is decisive: conscience cannot be a purely subjective thing—I follow my conscience, you follow yours! Obviously we expect that, in every conscience, Good will raise its hand to speak and Evil will be rejected. This is precisely what we presuppose when we appeal to someone's conscience. We expect that in his heart the voice of Good will become audible, that he will listen to this voice. We rouse his conscience and hope that he will heed its call. It deeply disturbs us when someone remains deaf to all appeals to conscience.

So we understand better what is said about conscience in the now well-known text of Vatican II: " 'Deep within his conscience man discovers a law which he has not laid upon himself but which he must obey. Its voice, ever calling him to love and to do what is good and to avoid evil, sounds in his heart at the right moment . . .'" (*GS* 16, quoted in CCC 1776).

In order to hear this voice, the conscience needs to be "well-formed" (CCC 1783). We feel that it is high moral praise when we can say of someone that he has "a delicate conscience". By this we mean that he is sensitive even to the faint stirrings of conscience. Such a man will be especially empathetic toward his neighbor.

Another part of forming conscience is distinguishing between genuine pangs of conscience and false feelings of guilt (CCC 1784): What really is the movement of the moral conscience, and what is only a reflection of current public opinion, the spirit of the age? Someone who feels bad because he cannot afford to spend as much as his neighbor more likely has false feelings of guilt. It would be better to have a bad conscience because he is not caring enough for his own family. A bad conscience is also a hopeful sign: I yearn to do better and hope that God will have mercy on me and my failure (CCC 1781). The more we recognize, in faith, how immeasurable God's mercy is, the deeper we can recognize, in our conscience, how much we are dependent upon that mercy.

# *Virtue*

Thus far we have asked what makes a deed, a human action, good. In pursuing this question we have hit upon several fundamental building stones of human morality: freedom, conscience, and the right decision, the right ordering of the passions. Yet we still do not have one essential building stone. What makes it possible for us to call good not only a particular deed but also the man himself? What constitutes the "good man"?

In this regard we must ask: Do good men exist at all? Does Jesus not say: "If you then, who are evil, know how to give good gifts to your children . . ." (Lk 11:13)? And· "Why do you call me good? No one is good but God alone" (Lk 18:19). "If we say we have no sin, we deceive ourselves" (1 Jn 1:8).

Of course this does not mean that in man there is nothing good at all, only bad. Jesus himself calls Nathanael a man "in whom is no guile" (Jn 1:47). And the Bible describes many people as being "righteous"—for instance, Saint Joseph (Mt 1:19), Zechariah and Elizabeth (Lk 1:6), and Simeon (Lk 2:28). That does not mean that they were completely without fault and free of all sin but, rather, that they were upright men, without guile, without the crooked and perverse traits that make men evil.

It is part of the fundamental understanding of the Christian image of man, of Catholic moral doctrine, that

God alone can be and is called "good" in the absolute, perfect sense, but that we human beings need not therefore be called "bad". To be is a good thing: that is the fundamental conviction of the Christian faith in God the Creator, in the goodness of his creation (CCC 299).

In the case of man, being good is, of course, not simply guaranteed by the fact that we as creatures participate in the goodness of God; we must also put it into action by our lives. What makes a man into a good man? Not just the fact that he exists, although every creature, as something created by God, has its innate goodness (CCC 339).

Being good in the case of man has to do also with the fact that he has acquired this attribute and cultivates it as something lasting and stable. This is precisely what the Christian (as well as the pre-Christian) tradition calls "virtue".

Today the word "virtue", according to the poet Paul Valéry, "is encountered only in the catechism and in comedy, in academics and in operettas". All the more reason not to put off rediscovering the great, profound meaning of this word.

Saint Thomas defines "virtue" quite simply: "It makes a man good." It causes him, not only to do this or that thing well, but to be good himself. By this is meant not simply the development of habits (after all, there are good ones, too, not only bad ones!) but that particular attitudes become second nature to us (CCC 1804). Such attitudes can be acquired through practice or received as a grace. These human and Christian virtues, the four cardinal virtues and the three theological virtues, provide the subjects for the next seven commentaries.

# *Prudence*

Of all the virtues, prudence is mentioned first. But that just goes to show again how difficult it is for us today to deal with the word and with the reality of the virtues. "Prudent" sounds rather negative; it reminds one of "prudish"—that is, overly modest, priggish—or "shrewd"—which can also mean cunning, calculating, sly. Would it not be better, in the face of such difficulties, to do without such easily misunderstood words as virtue or prudence? Still, words are not arbitrarily interchangeable. Where a word is lost, the reality that it signifies easily disappears from view as well.

Virtues are proficiencies. A craftsman who has mastered his trade or a person who can play the piano well has "proficiency", and he can exercise this skill smoothly and rapidly, even though it took a lot of effort to acquire. The moral virtues are proficiencies that enable us to do readily what is right, so that it becomes a matter of course and a source of joy (CCC 1804).

Prudence is the proficiency of grasping reality correctly and of deciding and acting accordingly: both aspects are part of prudence (the first is easily overlooked). To be able to act in a way that is morally good, we must grasp reality correctly. This aspect is pointed out by the philosopher Josef Pieper, to whom we owe a masterful little book about prudence (J. Pieper, *Traktat über die Klugheit* [*Prudence* (New York: Pantheon Books, 1959)];

also *Über das christliche Menschenbild* [Einsiedeln: Johannes Verlag, 1995]). Modern morality tends to proceed mainly from moral obligation, from the Commandments, from duty. It separates obligation from being, that is, duty is to be done because it is duty, not because it is appropriate behavior that does justice to reality. A different view is offered by classical Christian morality: In order to do good, we must know reality. "Someone who does not know how things really are cannot do good, either" (J. Pieper).

Prudent is the person who grasps reality accurately. Therefore another part of prudence is seeking good advice, that is, listening to those who are experienced and knowledgeable. Openness that is ready to learn—also and above all with respect to God and to his Word—is a component of prudence.

The second aspect of prudence consists of addressing the reality that has been correctly grasped in a way that is appropriate and right. This requires, first of all, careful consideration: thinking things over oneself and also discussing them with experienced people. This requires in particular the gift of distinguishing good advice from bad. Here it becomes evident how prudence and conscience go together (CCC 1806). Nevertheless, only the final step perfects prudence: when, after conscientious consideration of the reality and its demands, the right decision is made and is decisively put into action using the right means. For prudence, ultimately, is demonstrated only in the right deed that "hits the mark": "Look, judge, act"—that holds true for all virtues, which is why it is also true that prudence is the guide of all the other virtues.

# *Justice*

Among all the virtues that prudence guides, justice stands in the first place. It concerns right conduct toward one's neighbor. For the society of men, therefore, it is the fundamental attitude and way of acting. Justice gives to the neighbor what is due to him (CCC 1807). Since no man lives only for himself, the virtue that provides a firm foundation for living together as human beings is the fundamental virtue.

The shortest definition of justice goes: "To give to each his due." In the classical Catholic doctrine of the virtues, justice is developed along three lines:

First there is the elementary form of justice between individual persons. This is called *commutative justice*. Thus the employer owes the employee an appropriate wage; thus the employee owes the employer an appropriate amount of work. Parents owe to their children the support and attention due to them; children owe their parents due respect; spouses owe each other esteem and mutual assistance. Does all that not sound all too calculating, all too businesslike? Are love, mercy, goodness not more important than justice?

When we really think about things, of course, we cannot help viewing interpersonal relationships, too, in light of the mutual obligations involved. Mutual justice is not everything. Without love there is ultimately no justice, either. But likewise without fundamental justice there is no love. Helping the refugee in need is not only a matter of generosity and love of neighbor but, rather, and primarily, a duty under justice.

The second form of justice is the right conduct of society toward the individual. One speaks of *distributive justice*. This is the particular task of the political authority, the state, but of all smaller societies as well. What the individual cannot manage to do alone requires the help of society. Someone who has spent his life working in the service of society is justified in expecting that society will stand by him in sickness and in old age. If the means available to that great society of the state become more scarce, distributive justice must be especially vigilant in seeing to it that the weaker members are not unjustly burdened, that the strong do not spare themselves at the expense of the weak.

The third form of justice is that of the individual toward society as a whole. In Scholasticism this is called *legal justice*. The point here is that each one of us shares a responsibility for the common good and that this has priority over personal interests or the concerns of particular groups. We see today—in the crisis of the welfare state—even more clearly that we cannot simply expect society to provide government assistance for the individual, but that the state with its social programs can exist only if every individual contributes his part to the common welfare.

Much could be said about each of these three forms of justice. The important thing is that only all three together give a complete picture of justice. Another important thing: the just man, the man with the upright heart, is the prerequisite for all three. Society, the common good, thrives on such upright men. That is also why the most profound form of this virtue is the justice practiced toward God: that we "give God his due" (cf. CCC 1807), everything that we owe him; that is, all that we are and all that we have. It is from him that we have it, for "Infinite Thy vast domain / Everlasting is Thy reign" (first stanza of "Holy God, We Praise Thy Name").

# Fortitude

Evil exists. The power of evil exists. Good does not prevail by itself—automatically, so to speak. Saint Augustine (in *The City of God* 19, 4) says that "the great virtue of fortitude" gives "overwhelming evidence" of this. There is no justice without the willingness to accept toils, adversities, dangers, occasionally even persecutions as part of the bargain. This readiness to stand up for what is good, despite all opposition, we call fortitude.

The power of evil is frightening. Fear and anxiety are the normal human reactions to all that threatens us. The person lacking in fear is lacking an important "organ" that warns us of dangers. Someone who, because of pride or stupidity, sees no dangers seriously endangers himself and others. For this reason, recklessness is not a sign of fortitude but, rather, the opposite. Fortitude consists also, therefore, in finding the proper measure for courage, so that it does not lead to arrogance or to carelessness in the face of dangers.

In contrast, the chief purpose of fortitude is to ensure "firmness in difficulties and constancy in the pursuit of the good" (CCC 1808). Concretely, this means overcoming fear of the difficulties that get in the way of the good. There can be many forms and various levels of this fear. It can be justified or groundless, the response to a vague feeling or a very specific threat. Fortitude has a lot to do with putting our fears in order, with finding out what we really ought to fear and which anxieties we should overcome.

Fortitude has to do particularly with overcoming "human respect". It is all too easy to understand when someone, fearing for his job, remains silent about an injustice done to a colleague. Cares about family or about one's own security can lead in such cases to conflicts that trouble the conscience. In times of dictatorship such situations develop frequently, yet they occur regularly, in more or less dramatic form, in everyday life as well Where is due proportion to be found? Jesus himself declares what it is: "Do not fear those who kill the body but cannot kill the soul; rather fear him who can destroy both soul and body in hell" (Mt 10:28). We can lose everything: health, happiness, good name, property. To fear losing these things is human and right, yet this must not become a fear that decides everything. Only one thing is absolutely to be feared: that through our own fault we lose ourselves definitively, that we separate ourselves eternally from God, who is our life. "Never permit me to be separated from you", we pray silently before Holy Communion.

Fortitude, therefore, originates in "fear of the Lord", that loving concern about not squandering the most precious thing in our lives, the love of God. Martyrdom, therefore, is rightly considered to be the ultimate case of fortitude: better to give up worldly goods and bodily life than to deny God's fidelity and love.

At the same time, something that is true of all the virtues becomes clear: love is their true measure.

# *Temperance*

In fourth place among the cardinal virtues stands the virtue that is called *temperantia* in Latin. The words "temperature" and "temperament" contain the same word, *temperare*: to order, to arrange, to mix properly, but also to set limits, to moderate. *Zucht und Maß* (Discipline and moderation), therefore, was the title that Josef Pieper gave to his book devoted to this virtue.

All virtues have to do with due proportion and order: prudence concerns the right judgment of what is to be done; justice deals with the appropriate behavior toward others; fortitude has to do with being suitably heedless of self at the onset of difficulties. The virtue of temperance has to do with the proper measure in man's actions on his own behalf.

Where does this proper measure lie? The answer of Saint Thomas Aquinas may come as a surprise: in the faculty of reason! This is quite commonly misunderstood: it is not a question here of a paltry, utterly joyless average, a dispassionate rationality in those areas of life that are immediately concerned with self-preservation: in eating and drinking and in the sexual realm.

To be "reasonable" in matters of food and sexuality means something different, which on closer examination proves to be something great: it is a question of that measure which guards the powers of self-preservation from the self-destructive effects that they can always have, or—better yet, stated positively—which puts those powers into action according to their purpose of building up and developing the human being. It might surprise us to discover in this the nucleus of chastity and abstinence, with which *temperantia* deals. Unchastity and lack of restraint in relation to pleasure are not bad because the joys and delights of the senses are bad but because man can endanger and even destroy himself and others through them. There is an accurate indicator of whether or not we are being undisciplined or licentious about food and sexuality: genuine joy. It can occur only where the interests of self are not sought greedily in all sorts of sensuality, which only leads to the loss of self in the search for pleasure.

As if by a shadow, Christianity has been accompanied from the beginning by the danger of Manichaeism, which regards anything sensual, including food and sexuality, as bad per se. Paul already had to speak against this heresy: "Everything created by God is good, and nothing is to be rejected if it is received with thanksgiving" (1 Tim 4:4). The virtue of temperance, therefore, finds in this its proper measure and its goal: that everything created by God should be used also according to the mind of God. In this perspective the word "chastity" acquires a positive connotation that is scarcely heard anymore today. Temperance is the prerequisite that prevents us from seeking ourselves in all things, thereby misusing them for our own sake. It aims to make us "transparent", so that we can really appreciate each other and God's creation.

This, of course, includes ascetical practices, restrictions, moderation, presence of mind, and self-discipline

(CCC 1809). The original meaning of Christian fasting is found here: so that the heart may become free and pure, completely open to God and to others, and freed from self.

# 13

# Natural and supernatural virtues

After the four cardinal virtues, the Christian tradition lists the three theological virtues (CCC 1812): faith, hope, and charity. Four and three: the number seven has symbolic significance; it is the number of completion or perfection. Four, since time immemorial, has been considered the number of the world, of earthly reality: four points of the compass, four elements. Three is the divine number: God the Triune. The entire Cathedral of Saint Stefan in Vienna—like many other cathedrals—is built according to this key juxtaposition of four and three. Thus the construction itself is meant to express the fact that heaven and earth, God and man, meet each other here in Jesus Christ, the God-man.

Is that not just an arbitrary game? Can life with all its variety be captured in such numerical schemes? Certainly, there is something playful to these classifications, but nothing arbitrary. The division of the fundamental human attitudes into four natural and three supernatural, four that can be acquired by men and three that God alone can grant, corresponds to experiences that have stood the test of time and proved to be true. Let us have a look at this interplay.

Virtue needs to be learned, just like any skill, any human proficiency. Education has as its goal the edification or building-up of the human person, of character. Of course, we often have to deal with a distorted idea of virtue. Especially since the nineteenth century it has been seen as the opposite of pleasure and joy, as sheer duty that usually runs counter to one's inclinations. Completely different is the view of the great Christian Doctors. According to them, the virtues correspond to true and deep-seated human inclinations, which is why it is a joy to practice them (CCC 1810). The basis for this positive view of the virtues: the deepest desire of man is for the Good, because he springs from a good Creator and is created for happiness.

Of course, Christian moral teaching knows, too, that we human beings are "wounded by sin" (CCC 1811). That is why it requires strenuous effort to do good. That is why the totality of human life is a constant endeavor, especially in the many little decisions and adjustments of daily life, to make sure that this deep inclination toward good actually prevails against the many temptations and trials that life brings us. That is why we need help from above—grace, which strengthens and upholds us, protects and prompts us. That is why Christian moral teaching is convinced that no human life can be successful without the help of grace: without it our own powers are too weak, the temptations too strong.

Yet those are not the only reasons why we need grace. Man is "built" in such a way that he is held together only "from above", as the Gothic arch is held in place by the keystone. We are not created only for a successful earthly life. Only through participation in God's life is the life of human beings completely realized. The theological virtues, faith, hope, and charity, are called "theological" because it is through them that divine life takes root in our souls (CCC 1813). They cannot be "made" by us, only received—to be sure, not in a purely passive way, but in such fashion that we accept this gift and develop it. Only through faith, hope, and charity does human life really become a Christian life, a "Life in Christ" (title of part 3 of the CCC).

# 14

# Faith

Faith is the gateway to divine life. "Without faith it is impossible to please [God]" (Heb 11:6), since faith unites the soul to God, creating a living fellowship with him. The one who believes "touches" God. Because we cannot live without God, cannot gain eternal life, faith is necessary for salvation—which means for life itself (cf. Mk 16:16).

But what is faith? Is it not a lot weaker than knowledge? An opinion rather than a sure knowledge? And does not our world, which is built to such a large extent upon technology, expect the assurance of knowledge, for which the uncertainty of supposing or surmising or maintaining is not enough? Cardinal Ratzinger has demonstrated very nicely how a highly technological world demands precisely this human attitude of faith to a high degree. "All of us sooner or later use products of technology whose scientific basis is unknown to us: the statics of a high-rise building—who can double-check the calculations to make sure of it? The functioning of an elevator? . . . The reliability of the formula of a medication?" (Joseph Cardinal Ratzinger, *Auf Christus schauen. Einübung in Glaube, Hoffnung, Liebe* [Herder, 1989], 11–12 [English translation: *To Look on Christ: Exercises in Faith, Hope, and Love* (New York: Crossroad, 1991)]). We rely continually on the skills and knowledge of others who understand matters in their particular field, and we do it because experience tells us that as a rule we have good reason to be confident. "A society without trust cannot live" (ibid., 13). "Natural" faith is an expression of that mutual trust without which we could not live together or cope with the world at all.

Supernatural faith is the well-founded certainty, confirmed again and again by experience (one's own and that of many, many others), that we can trust God entirely and absolutely. If in our "everyday faith" we already rely constantly on the knowledge and skills of others, then it makes even more sense to rely on him who is all-knowing and almighty, who "created heaven and earth" and holds everything in his hand. "By faith 'man freely commits his entire self to God'" (CCC 1814, quoting *DV* 5). "*By faith*, man completely submits his intellect and his will to God" (CCC 143; cf. *DV* 5). This is no blind obedience but, rather, the expression of a loving confidence in him who, more than all creatures, is trustworthy.

On our own, we are not capable of this confident devotion to God, his revelation, and his will. "Faith is a gift . . ." (CCC 153), a grace freely bestowed by God. Still, this gift needs to be tended. Faith can grow or can diminish again, depending on whether we "keep the faith . . ." (CCC 1816) or endanger it (CCC 162). In order to strengthen faith, works are needed (CCC 1815), a life lived out of faith, bearing witness to the faith (CCC 1816). If we profess our loyalty to Christ, our faith will grow, and this growth is once again his gift.

Faith does not mean having "experiences". Many saints testify that they, too, experienced the dark night of faith (CCC 165), in which experience and feelings are for the most part silent, and only loving confidence remains. It is precisely in these dark hours that faith shines brightly, because it derives all its certainty from God's fidelity.

# 15

# Hope

When Cardinal Ratzinger published the book-length interview *The Ratzinger Report* in the year 1985, there was a storm of protest and indignation. He was accused of pessimism because he had portrayed the state of the faith [as the book was entitled in German] in colors that were at times quite somber. In his reply to this criticism, the Cardinal tried to elaborate on the actual difference between optimism pessimism, on the one hand, and hope–hopelessness on the other (Joseph Cardinal Ratzinger, *Auf Christus schauen. Einübung in Glaube, Hoffnung, Liebe* [Herder, 1989], 42–52 [English translation: *To Look on Christ: Exercises in Faith, Hope, and Love* (New York: Crossroad, 1991)]). There are people who have an optimistic temperament. They are inclined to be cheerful, confident, and not easily disheartened, whereas a pessimistic temperament is inclined to melancholy and to seeing the dark side of things. We are not responsible for our temperament, even though we help to form it by the way in which we lead our life.

Hope is something entirely different from mere optimism. It is directed with a certain confidence toward what is to come and is not yet present. It is, first of all, a human attitude without which there can be no human life: the sick person hopes for recovery; the lover, for the return of the beloved; those afflicted by war, for peace. In every life there are plenty of hopes, of a greater or lesser sort; someone who has no hope left at all—if that is even possible—cannot live, either. Is death also the death of all hope? If it has the last word, if earthly life is "the last chance" before nothingness, then there is no real hope, either; then hoping for a sunny Sunday to go hiking is only an illusion that conceals the hopelessness of inevitable death.

Hope, as the Christian faith understands it, always has to do with a hope reaching beyond death: "In hope he believed against hope", says Paul (Rom 4:18) about Abraham, the archetype of hope (CCC 1819). Against all indications—he was already advanced in age, as was Sarah, his wife—he believed in the promise of a son. Against all indications he trusted in the One who then granted him this son, and he was ready to sacrifice him.

Hope need not be optimistic. It soberly examines the difficulties and comes to understand the situation. It does not believe and does not expect that "progress" will create a paradise on earth, that one day on this earth technology and medicine, man's knowledge and power, will do away with suffering and death. Hope is set on God; it is anchored in Jesus Christ (Heb 6:19–20; CCC 1820); it is stirred up by the Holy Spirit. It "hopes for God from God", as Saint Bonaventure says.

God is the proper reason for hope; he is also its proper object. To that extent hope is not pessimistic. It overcomes the pessimistic view of the things of this world, however well-founded it may be, humanly speaking, because in faith it holds fast to the truth that God, who raised Jesus Christ from the dead, will be victorious over all death's victories. Therefore "[i]t affords us joy even under trial" (CCC 1820). "Rejoice in your hope, be patient in tribulation" (Rom 12:12). Because hope is directed toward the imperishable happiness of heaven, "it keeps man from discouragement; it sustains him during times of abandonment . . ." (CCC 1818). "Hope does not disappoint us" (Rom 5:5).

# 16

# *Charity*

"If I . . . have not love": The famous words of Saint Paul in the hymn to love (1 Cor 13) bear witness to the certitude that no part of human life has value and permanence if charity is lacking (CCC 1826). Of all the moral and theological virtues, it is the greatest (1 Cor 13:13).

The reason why this is so is given by Saint Catherine of Siena (1347–1380), whom the Church honors as a Doctor of the Church: "Without love the soul cannot live; she always wants to love something. After all, she is made out of the material of love, because I [the Lord] have created her out of love" (*Dialogue* 2, 1).

The most basic reason for everything is God's "plan of sheer goodness" in creating the world and man (CCC 1). Everything is created out of the material of love, that is, out of God's good will. The origin of everything is God's love, which desires to communicate itself (CCC 294). It is written of all creatures: "And God saw that it was good" (Gen 1:10). That is why love is, above all else, *assent*. Josef Pieper says: "Loving someone or something means finding him or it *probus*, the Latin word for 'good'. It is a way of turning to him or it and saying, 'It's good that you exist; it's good that you are in this world!' " (J. Pieper, *Faith, Hope, Love* [San Francisco: Ignatius Press, 1997], 163–64). And Gabriel Marcel, the French philosopher and poet, takes this idea further: "To love a human being means to say: You will not die."

But *is* everything love that goes by the name of love? There are many forms and distortions of love: Love for a child is a form of love distinct from erotic love, and both in turn are different from the love of friendship. All of these varieties can degenerate, can turn into imprisonment, tyranny, slavery. To insure that love for a child is in due proportion, it must be thoroughly shaped by the highest form of love, which the Bible calls *agape, caritas*: the theological virtue of charity (CCC 1822). Erotic love, which is good and willed by God, is preserved from sliding into the misuse of the other as a means to an end when *agape* thoroughly shapes *eros* (CCC 1827). *Agape* preserves the love of friendship from egotism, opens up the friendship to include God and neighbor.

In what, though, does this love consist, which is called a theological virtue because it goes beyond our merely human powers and is thus a gift of God's grace, and which is nevertheless required of us and, indeed, constitutes the first and greatest commandment (CCC 1823)?

It would be a misunderstanding to believe that the first three forms of love just mentioned were selfish, bound up with personal interests, while "theological charity" was purely disinterested. The first commandment tells us, after all, to love God totally and likewise to love our neighbor "as ourselves". Our love is never entirely selfless; indeed, it cannot and should not be so. As creatures who receive everything that we are and have, we always need love; yes, in every human heart lives an infinite need for love. Yet now we discover: this limitless yearning to be loved, that is, to be wanted and affirmed, can be stilled only if we ourselves love, give the gift of love.

The deeper we grow, with the help of the Holy Spirit, into a love for God and for neighbor, the wider our hearts become to receive love, until one day God fills them totally, boundlessly, with his Love.

Jesus shows us one place where charity must prove itself especially: love of enemy (CCC 1825): to affirm the one who is my enemy nonetheless, not in the evil that he does to me, but rather in the good that is within him as God's creature. That is the perfection of the love of Christ, who loved me so much that he died for me (Gal 2:20).

# 17

# The gifts of the Holy Spirit

In the previous short meditations we have spoken about the foundations of Christian morality: about man's final goal, the fullness of happiness, and about those human actions and attitudes through which we direct ourselves by free choice toward this goal. The virtues have a special task to perform in this, since they are those attitudes that have become second nature to a man, those good habits that make us ready and willing to do good deeds.

In Christian moral teaching, as developed by Saint Thomas Aquinas, for instance, the gifts of the Holy Spirit play a particular role, even though they are generally not well understood. Even the *Catechism* mentions them only briefly (CCC 1830–1831). What is their special importance? Why are they essential if the Christian life is to attain its full vitality and dynamism?

"All who are led by the Spirit of God are sons of God" (Rom 8.14). To allow oneself to be led by the Spirit, to live and work under his impetus: this is what actually constitutes "Life in Christ" (cf. the title of part 3 of the *Catechism*).

The *Catechism* formulates two core statements: The gifts of the Holy Spirit "are permanent dispositions which make man docile in following the promptings of the Holy Spirit" (CCC 1830); and: "They make the faithful docile in readily obeying divine inspirations" (CCC 1831). What does this mean?

To act in a way that is morally right means to be led by reason, prudently to set a course headed for what is appropriate. We have received freedom from God so that we might choose the good ourselves. Without freedom there would be no responsibility either, and the latter in turn requires insight and foresight. Now our freedom is displayed not only in actively doing and governing, but also in assenting to God's deeds and governance. To allow oneself to be led by God, to abandon oneself to his direction, is the highest expression of our freedom.

The spiritual masters like to use a vivid image: When we hold our life in our own hands, it is like a boat that we row with our own strength; when we leave the direction of our lives to God, then it is like a sailboat with billowing sails that easily glides along. The gifts of the Holy Spirit enliven all our abilities and actions from within, more powerfully and easily than all our own efforts could ever manage.

This working of the gifts—according to Isaiah 11:2 there are seven of them—often becomes particularly clear in the lives of simple people. It may be that someone has acquired prudence and wisdom through much studying or else through experience in life. The gift of wisdom or that of counsel, however, means more: a spiritual sense, an "instinct of the Holy Spirit", which enables one to see things and situations in the light of God and not only within the parameters of human wisdom and prudence. In the lives of the saints we see how this "spiritual instinct", this sensitivity to the will of God, leads those who are led by the Spirit of God far beyond merely human standards of virtue. The gifts of the Holy

Spirit are the things that actually constitute the adventure of Christian life: that the surprising newness, freshness, and liveliness of the Holy Spirit is effective, even in the smallest everyday things.

# 18

# *What is sin?*

On our way thus far through Christian morality we have encountered principally the positive elements, the building stones of a successful moral life. No human life, however, is without the experience of dysfunctional behavior, of mistakes being made, of failure. And in the same way experience teaches us that we are not dealing here simply with technical difficulties in a malfunctioning human life, but often with moral offenses, too, for which we ourselves are to blame and hence must also be responsible. We speak then about "sin" (CCC 386).

What is sin? Is there such a thing at all? Is an awareness of sin just something that we are talked into, the after-effect of being brought up in a church, the result of anxious religiosity? Philosophers and psychologists have tried to "unmask" sin as merely the inculcation (or imagination) of religious claims to power over man. In the face of so much cruelty, of so much deliberate and ingeniously calculated evil in the twentieth century, it would be naïve to want to deny the reality of sin. But what is sin?

First: a misdeed, the breaking of a rule. "Traffic violation"—this expression indicates that there actually is today an awareness that breaking rules, for instance, while driving, can be something like a sin. Sin is a violation of the order of creation, which finds its expression in the Commandments. Unlike the orderliness of traffic, the order of creation is not something that man determines. It is presented to us as reality, designed and willed by the Creator. When we act and live in keeping with it, our interior and exterior life is in order. Happiness and joy testify for us to this conformity with God and his work.

The disorder of sin comes about when we are biased and cling to certain things, when, for instance, only the fruit from the forbidden tree appears desirable and all other goods, the permitted fruits of the garden, are as if forgotten (Gen 3:1–7). Forgotten or repressed also is the voice of God, which makes itself known in the conscience, in God's instructions. Sin, therefore, is intrinsically and essentially turning one's back on God, looking away from him and refusing to hear him: "Like the first sin, it is disobedience, a revolt against God through the will to become 'like gods' [Gen 3:5]" (CCC 1850).

The essence of sin is demonstrated by the fact that we can never sin "with our whole hearts", with all our strength, "without interior reservations" (J. Pieper, *Über den Begriff der Sünde* [On the concept of sin] [Munich: Kösel, 1977], 52). Only in the realm of good can we be entirely ourselves, dedicate ourselves with all our strength. When we are caught up in evil we are never at one with ourselves but, rather, are torn between what we are doing—against our better, reasonable judgment, against our conscience (which perhaps is only speaking softly) and in estrangement from God—and what we recognize as being good and contributing toward our happiness (CCC 1849).

Another aspect of sin, though, is that it makes us blind to these connections. The drama of sin is that it inclines and compels a person to make excuses for himself (cf. Gen 3:8–13). The greatest danger is the hardening of the heart, impenitence. Only the Holy Spirit can uncover sin in such a way that being convicted of sin leads to liberating conversion, to the joy of forgiveness (CCC 1848).

# Grave sin—light sin

The fact that sin does not always have the same gravity is generally recognized. There is a difference between killing someone and stealing a little money from someone. As soon as we try, though, to determine more precisely what actually constitutes serious sin, it becomes difficult. Besides, many things used to be described as "mortal sins" that today are scarcely perceived as being even venial sins.

According to the traditional teaching, three conditions must be met, together, in order for an act to count as a mortal sin: " 'Mortal sin is sin whose object is grave matter and which is also committed with full knowledge and deliberate consent' " (*RP* 17 § 12, quoted in CCC 1857). In view of this definition, one might ask whether it is possible at all to commit a grave or mortal sin. Certainly, there are sins that are grave with respect to their object: murder, apostasy [falling away from the faith], adultery, and so on. But what about the other two conditions? Who ever sins seriously "with full knowledge"? Saint Thomas says, "Blindness is, so to speak, a prerequisite for sin" (*Summa theologiae* I–II, 79, 3). Does not Jesus himself pray, when confronted with the most serious sin ever committed by man, the slaying of the Son of God: "Father, forgive them; for they know not what they do" (Lk 23:34)? If they do not know what they do, though, then the third condition is not fulfilled: "with deliberate consent", that is, sinning with a will that is entirely free. And yet there is no getting around Jesus' clear statement: "If you were blind, you would have no guilt" (Jn 9:41).

Is there such a thing as a "blind seeing", a seeing and yet not perceiving (cf. Mk 4:12)?

Perhaps that is the most awful "mystery of lawlessness" (2 Thess 2:7), that we can become blind to evil with our eyes open. The rich glutton is threatened with eternal ruin because he no longer even notices poor Lazarus at his door. He does not deliberately refuse to give bread to the poor man; rather, he does not see Lazarus any more, because his life of luxury has blinded him. According to the description of the Last Judgment (Mt 25:31–46), it is not the deliberate sins of commission that lead to eternal damnation but, rather, the neglectful sins of omission: "I was hungry and you gave me no food" (Mt 25:42).

"Feigned ignorance and hardness of heart [cf. Mk 3:5–6; Lk 16:19–31] do not diminish, but rather increase, the voluntary character of a sin" (CCC 1859).

What, then, makes a grave sin a "mortal" sin (cf. 1 Jn 5:16–17), which endangers a man's soul to the point of jeopardizing the eternal salvation for which he was predestined? The answers given by the great Christian masters are helpful here: Sin, at its core, consists of turning away from God, turning to myself. It is " 'love of oneself even to contempt of God' " (Saint Augustine, *De civitate Dei* 14, 28: PL 41, 436, quoted in CCC 1850). The same masters see the difference between grave and light sins, mortal and venial sins, in their respective consequences: the former destroy love of God, while the latter "only" injure it.

That is why only a new, profound conversion and the grace of God can awaken a soul out of mortal sin, whereas venial sins can be healed through a fresh outpouring of love. However, many small, thoughtless acts of unkindness can kill love (CCC 1863); many light sins can have grave consequences. The magnificent remedy that the Lord has given us is the opportunity to confess our sins and so to convert our hearts again to love (CCC 1458).

# *Community*

On our way thus far through Christian morality we have dealt mainly with the good or bad actions or attitudes of the individual. The *Catechism* follows exactly the structure of the Pastoral Constitution of the [Second Vatican] Council when it now widens its perspective to consider the human community, which is necessary for the development of the individual (CCC 1877).

The biblical and Christian view of the relationship between the individual and the community (or, in the more comprehensive sense, society) has two "poles", which give the full picture only when they are taken together. Man has a communal character. From the moment of his conception on, he lives in relationships with others and needs community: with his own mother, his father, his brothers and sisters. The family is thus the first, natural community of every human being.

Other forms of community are then added: language, culture, religion, country, nation, state, and so on. Hence living in relation to others, belonging to communities, is not something that is added to man extraneously, more or less by chance, and that he could do without.

It is important today to recall this clearly, since the prevailing view of man is strongly individualistic, and being single has practically become the decisive model of society.

It follows that human communities are not simply

conglomerations of individuals. There is something about them that "goes beyond each one . . ." of their members (CCC 1880). Communities and societies are held together by something greater that transcends the individual. Language, for instance, is a common heritage that unites us, and we in turn cooperate in handing it on. Traditions of law, of social conduct, of culture, and of religion are instances of basic communal givens without which the individual could not exist at all. They entail at the same time a duty to foster them, to pass them on and to develop them further. Since we are all supported by communities, we also owe it to the community to carry our share of the load: we bear responsibility for it.

Still, the second pole must immediately be mentioned. However true it may be that we are communal beings, it is just as true that the individual, as a person, is not completely dissolved in the community. The person, with his eternal destiny and in his inexpressible dignity, transcends all communal ties. " '[T]he *human person* . . . is and ought to be the principle, the subject and the end of all social institutions' " (GS 25 § 1, quoted in CCC 1881). We never belong entirely to the family, to the nation, to the state. Man entirely belongs only to God. No institution can make a total claim upon the human person.

Individualism forgets about relatedness to the community; collectivism (toward which dictatorships tend) denies the transcendent dignity of the person. Catholic social teaching constantly strives to renew an awareness of both of these poles.

This is no naïve, otherworldly view. We see clearly

today how important a prerequisite the unconditional dignity of the individual person is for a humane society for all—the unborn and the elderly, the weak and the well—and how necessary, on the other hand, a distinct sense of community is so that our society does not become cold and inhuman.

# 21

# *Authority*

Authority comes from God. This is what the Church teaches, and she bases her teaching both on Sacred Scripture and also on human reason. To many people today this is a strange and barely comprehensible idea. "Authority" is to a great extent understood negatively, at best it is taken to mean the "delegation" of authority, a commission made by the people, proceeding from the grass roots.

Paul merely summarizes what the Sacred Scriptures say in many places: "There is no authority except from God, and those that exist have been instituted by God" (Rom 13:1). How are we to understand this? Does this view not stem from a "pre-democratic" world, in which the ruler governed by the grace of God and not on behalf of the voters?

Let us begin with a fact that is evident to most people: "Every human community needs an authority to govern it" (CCC 1898; cf. Leo XIII, *Immortale Dei*; *Diuturnum illud*): No orchestra can function without a conductor, no business without a boss, no government without a leader, regardless of whether the person in charge was chosen by all or by a few, or whether that person was appointed by those in higher positions. Without a leading authority, chaos or caprice rules, and so the community cannot flourish, a common undertaking cannot succeed. A "boss" proves himself to be an "authority" when the good of those entrusted to his care is promoted under his direction. The word "authority" comes from the Latin *auctoritas*. *Augere* means to grow. "Authority" is that quality of persons which promotes growth and removes obstacles, always with a view to the good of the individual and of the community.

This, of course, requires certain parameters and conditions: Whoever holds authority—whether in the family, in the working world, in politics—must not use it arbitrarily (CCC 1902). To be able to command, it is not enough merely to have the power to command; the legitimate and just exercise of authority is necessary as well. Unjust laws and morally illicit commands destroy authority and cannot be binding in conscience. Here the rule applies: "We must obey God rather than men" (Acts 5:29). "In such a case, 'authority breaks down completely and results in shameful abuse' ", says Pope John XXIII (CCC 1903, quoting *PT* 51).

That is why it is so important for laws and institutions to be guided by the objective moral order, by the divine law. Just as much harm can result from unjust laws, from sinful structures (CCC 1869), as from the personal abuse of power.

Not even the best authority is of any use, of course, if the respect due to it is not shown. Today we too easily forget that we also owe gratitude and recognition to those who bear the burden and responsibility of authority and, last but not least, prayers that they will have the help of God, from whom all good authority is ultimately derived.

# 22

# *The common good*

Every man strives for happiness; each person is urged on toward "self-realization", that is, the development of one's own life, the fulfillment of one's own desires. How is this striving supposed to fit in with the requirements of the community? Indeed, there is not just the welfare of the individual but also that of the community to think about. How are they related to each other? Does the good of the community come about only when the individual is compelled (by laws and controls) to give up his individualism, as "collectivism" sees it? Or does the right equilibrium between individual and community result when people strive for the greatest possible good for the greatest possible number, as "liberalism" supposes?

Yet what is happiness? What does it consist of? And what is the common good, the welfare of the community? What do they consist of?

The Christian view is like an ellipse with two foci. The first focus is the certitude, derived from revelation, that man has a dignity transcending that of any community: the person is created by God in his image and is destined for God, for eternal happiness in a perfectly fulfilling communion with God. It is toward this ultimate and most exalted goal of man that everything else is ordered and should be ordered.

Yet this goal is not realized individualistically. God

himself—even though this is an unfathomable mystery—is a "community" of Persons within himself. None of us arrives at his goal alone. This is true already in the natural realm of earthly life, and it is even more true of the supernatural goal of eternal life.

That is why the good of the individual and the good of the community are intimately interwoven. Personal fulfillment is attained more easily and more fully when the right social conditions are present (CCC 1906). There are chiefly three essential elements that constitute the common good:

—*unconditional respect for the human person:* Never to this day has a regime that despises human beings (even if it despises "only" particular groups of people) furthered the common good in the long run. Respect for the human person is indispensable; only a society founded upon this principle can flourish (CCC 1907).

—*the social well-being of the community:* An equitable balance between the interests of individuals and those of groups is the prerequisite for a society in which the necessities of life are and remain accessible to all (CCC 1908).

—*peace:* "that is, the stability and security of a just order" (CCC 1909). We often realize what a precious thing freedom is only when it is lost.

So we understand why Saint Thomas describes the common good as being nothing short of "divine", that is, as the most precious good for the individual as well as for the community. Hence employing all available forces for the sake of the common good is the supreme duty. Hence we owe recognition and thanks to all those who in a special way stand up for the common good.

# 23

# Equality and diversity

There are few questions so difficult to address today as
that of equality and diversity among us as human beings.
For it is important today to make both things very clear
again: that all men truly have equal dignity and that all
men are different, that no one is simply equal to another. How can we describe the correct relationship
between these two aspects?

It is worth rereading today the first encyclical of Pope
Pius XII, dated October 1939, in which he explained
with utmost clarity why the Church can never accept
the National-Socialist doctrine about race: humanity
constitutes a family that has its origin in God; all men,
without exception, share in the same human nature; the
earth is entrusted to all men alike as a place to live
[*Lebensraum*]; common to all is life's supernatural goal—
eternal life with God; all have the same Redeemer, Jesus
Christ, who died and rose from the dead for all men
(CCC 360; 1939).

Seen from this Christian perspective, " '[e]very form
of . . . discrimination . . . on the grounds of sex, race,
color, social conditions, language, or religion must be
curbed and eradicated as incompatible with God's design' " (*GS* 29 § 2, quoted in CCC 1935).

Just as important, though, is the other aspect: No
human being is simply equal to another; there are countless differences that are just as much in keeping with

God's design as is the equal dignity of all men. Certainly there are unjust inequalities, which contradict the spirit of the Gospel (CCC 1938), but it is important today to rediscover that the countless differences between human beings also have something to do with God's plan. The first difference is mentioned on the first page of the Bible: man and woman are of equal dignity; both are created in the image of God (cf. Gen 1:26); yet they are created different, in body and soul, so as to complement and help one another (cf. Gen 2:18), so that each might make a distinctive personal contribution to the common work. What would the world be without this difference between man and woman, the source of so much mutual enrichment and, yes, of so many conflicts, which, however, do not result from the diversity, but rather from our lack of conversion (CCC 1916). What would the Church be without this mutual complementarity of man and woman?

Then there are the differences among the infinitely varied talents, experiences, character traits, physical abilities, the differences of age, of health, and also those of moral behavior. All of these differences demand different approaches as well. The fact that all must contribute to the common good does not mean that all must contribute the same thing; rather, that we all have to rely on one another. The differences signify mutual dependence. They remind us of our fundamental dependence upon God, before whom each one is accountable for the talents he has received.

# 24

# *The law*

"I will delight in your statutes; I will not forget your word" (Ps 119:16). This is the prayer of the longest psalm, which is one extended song in praise of God's law—an expression of the yearning to follow it entirely and absolutely.

Delight in the law: that is not so easy for us to understand, because in modern times we all too easily view the law as constraint, as something external restricting our freedom, like a corset. Judaism, on the other hand, observes year after year the Simchas Torah (the Rejoicing of the Law), which is celebrated by dancing in the synagogue with the scroll of the Torah, as though with a bride. Certainly, the reason why God's law is also perceived as a constraint is that we ourselves are alienated from God by sin, and it is not possible to return to him without painful conversion. But in itself the law is extremely delightful, joyful, and reasonable. So what is the significance of the law?

On our way toward our goal, beatitude, our own powers—reason and will, virtues and motives—are not sufficient by themselves. We need God's help. It comes to us "through the law that guides [us] . . . and the grace that sustains [us]" (CCC 1949).

God's law is not something arbitrary, the incomprehensible imposition of a blind force. Rather, we find it first of all in ourselves, as the light of reason. In this light

" 'we know what we must do and what we must avoid' " (Saint Thomas Aquinas, *Collationes in decem praeceptis*, I, quoted in CCC 1955). In our faculty of reason we "hear" the law as the expression of the reason of the Creator, who gave to all things their order and, to us, the light of reason that makes it possible to perceive this order in us and all around us.

The "moral law" written in the heart of every man, therefore, is an echo and an expression of the "eternal law" of God himself (CCC 1951): " 'Theft is surely punished by your law, O Lord, and by the law that is written in the human heart, the law that iniquity itself does not efface' " (Saint Augustine, *Confessions* 2, 4, 9: PL 32, 678, quoted in CCC 1958). We know that, all over the earth, every man hears the voice of God's law in his own heart—at least in principle—and that this is and has been and will be so at all times.

This natural law is the foundation of all human coexistence; despite all cultural diversity and variations in circumstances, it is *"immutable"* (CCC 1958): a lie remains always a lie, for the Eskimos as it is for us, in ancient Rome as in the New World.

That does not mean that the moral law is always and everywhere perceived with the same clarity. In the life of the individual as well as of the community there is also a certain loss of vision in moral matters. Thus today very often—at least so it appears—the killing of children in their mother's wombs is no longer perceived as such.

That is why we need the revelation of the law. The Ten Commandments summarize the things that in themselves ought to be clear to us in our hearts: " 'God wrote on the tables of the Law what men did not read in their hearts' " (Saint Augustine, *Enarrationes in Psalmos* 57, 1: PL 36, 673, quoted in CCC 1962). This "reminder" should not remain external: God wants to place his living law so deep in our hearts that it becomes the inmost driving force of our will.

This happens when Christ, through the Holy Spirit, becomes "our law of life".

# 25

# Grace

Paul usually greets his communities with the following good wishes: "Grace to you and peace from God our Father and the Lord Jesus Christ" (2 Cor 1:2). Grace is one of the principles of our faith. It is also, however, one of the forgotten or at least neglected words in the Christian vocabulary. Many are of the opinion that it would be better not to use it at all, since it is scarcely comprehensible today. To do without a word of such central importance to our faith, however, would mean gradually losing sight of the thing it designates. When Paul wishes grace, at the outset, to the Christian communities, it means that the most important thing is being mentioned here.

The word grace means first of all—in secular usage as well—something unearned, which one has no right to claim. To pay the just wage is not to show favor toward an employee but is, rather, the employer's duty under justice. It is quite different with a gift, which is given of one's own accord. Grace, furthermore, means benevolence, favor, although today it may sound rather condescending to be "benevolent" or "gracious".

When we speak of God's grace, we mean the "*favor, the free and undeserved help* that God gives us to respond to his call . . ." (CCC 1996). This definition addresses something essential in our relationship to God: the fact that we cannot assert any sort of right or claim before

God. We are entitled in God's sight neither to our existence nor to happiness. Maybe the reason why there is a certain allergy to the word "grace" is that it clearly expresses our total dependence upon God in our relations with him.

Grace, however, also means benevolence, attentiveness, help, deliverance. All this is plentifully, superabundantly promised to us, unearned, undeserved; even more—not only promised, but also bestowed, given to us personally as a gift. God created us not only for our earthly life, but for his divine life. We actually receive a share in it. "The grace of Christ is the gratuitous gift that God makes to us of his own life . . ." (CCC 1999), a real participation in God's life—this is what grace accomplishes and bestows. The Christian life really begins only when it is lived in this supernatural dimension (CCC 1998), when God's gift becomes the foundation of our lives, on the basis of which we no longer think and act in a merely "natural" way but live by the Spirit of Christ, as branches on the true Vine (CCC 1988).

Grace does not deprive us of freedom or make us God's "marionettes". It makes us God's free co-workers (CCC 1993), who—this is a great but utterly real mystery—respond freely and with joy to the slightest directions and promptings of the Holy Spirit (CCC 2002). It is characteristic of grace that it even grants us our willing: "For God is at work in you, both to will and to work for his good pleasure" (Phil 2:13).

Grace takes many forms. It is helpful to name the various aspects of grace by their proper names: sanctifying grace, which justifies us and makes us children of God (CCC 1987); habitual grace, that is, the grace that works as a permanent disposition (may we never lose it!); and actual graces, both prevenient and concomitant [that is, going before and following upon our good decisions] (CCC 2000f.), sacramental graces and the graces of state, the special graces that are called charisms (CCC 2003–2004). The experience of Christian life says, with the Little Flower, Saint Thérèse: "Everything is grace!"

# 26

# Merit

This word—as part of the vocabulary of faith—has become even more unfamiliar than grace. Still, the difficulties of understanding it should not be overestimated. Nowadays we are probably too timid about using the language of faith. On closer examination it becomes evident that most of the fundamental words of our faith have a secular basis that is readily understood. In his parables the Lord always speaks of worldly realities in order to make the things of the kingdom of heaven understandable.

Jesus often promises a "reward in heaven": "Blessed are you when men revile you and persecute you . . . on my account. Rejoice and be glad, for your reward is great in heaven" (Mt 5:11–12). "Lay up for yourselves treasures in heaven, where neither moth nor rust consumes and where thieves do not break in and steal. For where your treasure is, there will your heart be also" (Mt 6:20–21).

Merit and reward: these are first of all everyday realities. "The laborer deserves his wages" (Lk 10:7); if someone has performed a meritorious service, we owe him recompense. If merits are not honored, then that is not only ungratefulness but also injustice (CCC 2006). This is true not only of material but also of spiritual achievements. When we speak of a "highly meritorious personage", we mean someone who with selfless dedication has done much for others, for the common good. No doubt there is also something like "storing up merits" in this life; in this regard the Lord points out to us that it is not a matter of being "rewarded" by men: Let your alms "be in secret; and your Father who sees in secret will reward you" (Mt 6:4).

Does God therefore owe us a reward when we do good? Before God can there be such a thing as merit at all? Is it not all grace, an unearned and undeserved gift (CCC 2007)? As in all questions of faith, Christian experience helps to give an answer here, too. The saints make it clear that precisely those good works, those "merits", appeared to them to be, not their own achievements but, rather, gifts of God's grace. The saints have always had the awareness that they stand before God "with empty hands" (Saint Thérèse of Lisieux). All that they have and accomplish they consider as the work of God (CCC 2011).

Yet it is thoroughly characteristic of grace that it empowers us to cooperate in God's work. Christ has made us his friends. He has entrusted to us all that he has received from the Father. Thus we are really "co-heirs" with Christ and are able to obtain "merits" with him, through him, and in him (CCC 2009). Since we have everything from him, our merits also remain the work of his grace.

These considerations make the Church's teaching and practice concerning indulgences (CCC 1471–1479) more comprehensible; today it is commonly unknown and often misunderstood. Since no one lives for himself alone, the graces and merits of one soul are always a blessing for the others, too, in the communion of saints.

"In this wonderful exchange, the holiness of one profits others, well beyond the harm that the sin of one could cause others" (CCC 1475). "Indulgence" means that the merits of Christ and his saints are applied to us, the living and the deceased, to heal the traces of sin that we carry within us. We should lay claim more often to this solidarity, for ourselves as well as for others.

# 27

# Called to holiness

Our short expedition through the elements of Christian morality (which theologians call "fundamental morals") is at an end. The *Catechism* has organized these elements and presented them in an arrangement that takes its orientation both from Saint Thomas Aquinas and also from the Second Vatican Council.

Setting out from the final goal of man, his happiness, which he can find only in God, we first considered human acts and attitudes (works and virtues), by which we, as individuals and in community, strive to attain our final goal but also to reach the concrete intermediate goals in a conducive manner, in a way that is morally good. Part of the Christian message, though, is that we can reach neither particular goals nor our final goal by our own strength alone. Without God's external and internal help, without his law and his grace, we are hopelessly lost. This is a truth of the faith, strictly speaking. Jesus answers the uneasy question of his disciples: "Who then can be saved?": "With men this is impossible, but with God all things are possible" (Mt 19:25–26). But in the same way it is an indisputable truth of the faith that God "desires all men to be saved and to come to the knowledge of the truth" (1 Tim 2:4). Even more: God wills that, through his Son, all men "become, in the Holy Spirit, his adopted children and thus heirs of his blessed life" (CCC 1).

The Council says nothing else but this when it speaks about the universal call to holiness (CCC 2013). The goal of human life is divine life. We find the deepest fulfillment, not in ourselves, but in God. Only in God will we be entirely ourselves. Then the commandment that Jesus gave us is fulfilled: "You, therefore, must be perfect, as your heavenly Father is perfect" (Mt 5:48).

But what is holiness? It begins when there is cooperation between our actions and God's working, when we comply with God's word and prompting and, by his help, allow ourselves to be led by him. How does that happen? Only through love that is lived day by day. Claire de Castelbajac, a radiant figure who has beome a model for many young people (she died at the early age of twenty-one on January 22, 1975), wrote: "Holiness is the love of living entirely commonplace things for God and with God, by his grace and his power." There is no other way to holiness than that of love, and this way is open to all, in every state of life and in every age. This is the real "equal opportunity" in the Church. Only along this way does the Church renew herself. " 'The saints have always been the source and origin of renewal in the most difficult moments in the Church's history' " (John Paul II, *CL* 16, 3, quoted in CCC 828).

The way of holiness, of concrete love for God and for neighbor in all situations of life, leads through the narrow gate of the Cross. "There is no holiness without renunciation and spiritual battle" (CCC 2015; cf. 2 Tim 4). Yet we do not wage this battle with our own forces; the entire history of the Old Covenant teaches us that, precisely when the people of God discovered its own weakness, it also experienced God's helping hand. The experience of Saint Paul is no different: "When I am weak, then I am strong" (2 Cor 12:10). To become holy does not mean doing quite extraordinary things but, rather, continually allowing Christ to tell me: "My grace is sufficient for you, for my power is made perfect in weakness" (2 Cor 12:9). None of us, therefore, can say, Holiness is too high for me to reach!

# 28

# Magisterium and morality

Before turning in the next sections to the Ten Commandments, let us reflect upon a question that is often disputed today: Is it the Church's business to make binding pronouncements in questions of morality? The *Catechism* addresses this subject at the conclusion of the general discussion of Christian morality (CCC 2030–2051).

The answers to this question are contradictory. In many areas "the Church" (whereby the Magisterium is meant, especially the teaching authority of the Pope) is accused of interfering too much. On the other hand, the Church is expected to have and to be a "moral authority".

Now there are plenty of examples, in both the history and the current situation of the Church, where moral credibility has been lacking. At the same time, within the Church inexhaustible sources of renewal are flowing. Why do we have so little confidence in pointing to the moral strength of the Church? In the midst of the horrible War, Pius XII recalled it: " 'For two thousand years this sentiment has lived and endured in the soul of the Church, impelling souls then and now to the heroic charity of monastic farmers, liberators of slaves, healers of the sick, and messengers of faith, civilization, and science to all generations and all peoples for the sake of creating the social conditions capable of offering to everyone possible a life worthy of man and of a Christian'" (Discourse, June 1, 1941, quoted in CCC 1942).

The Church first "proclaims morality", therefore, not by the words of her preaching and the codifying of her doctrine, but rather by the witness of her life (CCC 2044). "The Church increases, grows, and develops through the holiness of her faithful . . ." (CCC 2045). Example is attractive. Should that not be enough? What is the Magisterium for? Why does it have authority? For no other reason than the one that led in the Old Covenant to the writing down of God's law and his Commandments: "'God wrote on the tables of the Law what men did not read in their hearts'" (Saint Augustine, *Enarrationes in Psalmos* 57, 1: PL 36, 673, quoted in CCC 1962). In and of themselves, the light of reason shines clearly enough and the voice of conscience speaks clearly enough for us to recognize God's Commandments. Yet our perception and our will have been weakened by sin. The Church has no "new morality" to proclaim; rather she has to remind us about moral principles of lasting validity (CCC 2036). That is why the Church speaks, in questions of medical ethics, economics, and communication, not only for the faithful but for all men (CCC 2032).

In all these questions it is always a matter of man as well, of his well-being and his salvation. The Church is, as Pope Paul VI put it, an "expert in humanity".

The Church is also entrusted with the Gospel, though, with Christ's Good News of salvation. This "New Law" (CCC 1965) is written on our hearts when we allow the Holy Spirit to lead us. So that we would not go astray, Christ willed that his Church would never be without a sure compass to indicate the right direction. The infallibility of the teaching authority of the Pope and the bishops with him—extending to all those things that are essential and necessary to the life of faith—keeps the Church, therefore, on the way of Christ, which is often fogbound by the spirit of the age and darkened by our willfulness (CCC 2034–2035). So it is no surprise that the Pope is often perceived as a "sign of contradiction", precisely in questions of morality.

# 29

# *The Ten Commandments*

The *Catechism* makes use of the Ten Commandments as a framework for presenting Christian morality. Some have objected to this, saying that we live in the New Covenant, after all, and are no longer obliged by the Old Testament Law of the Ten Commandments but rather by the "new commandment" of love. Others have thought that, within Christianity, we should choose faith, hope, and charity as the basis for the Christian life. Nevertheless, the Decalogue (which means the "ten words", cf. CCC 2056) was deliberately and decisively chosen to present the concrete demands of an upright human and Christian life.

There are good reasons for this choice. Jesus himself referred again and again to the Ten Commandments: "If you would enter life, keep the commandments" (Mt 19:17). The Commandments are instructions for living, and nothing could be more misguided than to conclude from the negative formulation ("you shall not . . .") that they are merely a list of prohibitions. They show us the way of life; they keep us from the ways of death. What they command and what they warn against can be understood in principle by every man through the light of his reason.

C. S. Lewis, in his masterful little book *The Abolition of Man* (the book first appeared during the Second World War), prophetically predicted the dramatic consequences that result from the denial of objective, valid criteria for truth and morality. By this denial, man to a certain extent abolishes himself. When good and evil, true and false, are only a matter of personal preference, only "a question of taste", this leads to the destruction not only of the community but of the human personality as well. To affirm the universal validity of the Ten Commandments, C. S. Lewis cites a wealth of examples from a wide variety of cultures and religions, which testify to the general acknowledgment of the natural law. Of course, C. S. Lewis also explains that the fundamental order expressed in the Ten Commandments is not valid because it is found and acknowledged everywhere in the world, but rather the reverse: it meets with recognition in so many peoples and religions because it is right and true. That is why the Ten Commandments are a serious obligation for all men, always and everywhere (CCC 2072).

Why, then, were the Ten Commandments revealed by God so solemnly, if they are already written in the heart of man and are evident to his reason? "Keep the Commandments" as a way of life—that means more than leading a "reasonable" life. In the first place, it is a matter of living in covenant, in communion with God. God's Commandments usually begin with "I am the LORD . . ." and then conclude: "You shall. . . ." Keeping the Ten Commandments is the response to God's holiness (CCC 2062). Because we have been received into a covenant, our whole life should be stamped with fidelity to God. "Keep the Commandments"—that means, intrinsically, clinging to God with our whole heart. That is why the twofold commandment of love is also the fulfilling of the law (CCC 2055).

To the rich young man Jesus says: "If you would be perfect, . . . come, follow me" (Mt 19:21). A life lived according to the Ten Commandments is good; it is a way to true life. Christ, though, wants more. The Beatitudes go further; the Sermon on the Mount demands more—not only to refrain from killing, but to love one's enemies (CCC 2054).

When we follow him, he himself becomes the guideline of our conduct; he lives and loves in us (CCC 2074).

# 30

# You shall believe in one God

"I am the Lord your God"—so begins the catechetical formula in which the first commandment has long been handed down and learned. "You shall have no other gods before me" are the exact words found further on in both Old Testament versions of the Ten Commandments (Exodus 20 and Deuteronomy 5). The core of the statement of prohibition is the positive summons to love God alone and with all one's might. What this entails, but also excludes, has to be shown in an explanation of the first commandment.

The first commandment is the fundamental one. In it all the others are contained as though in a nucleus, just as in the first article of the Creed all the subsequent ones are included: "I believe in God" (CCC 199): "For whoever would draw near to God must believe that he exists and that he rewards those who seek him" (Heb 11.6). Believing in God is the first requirement for a good, moral life as well as for right thinking and feeling. *Dieu premier servir*, "To serve God first" was the motto of Saint Joan of Arc. She summed up the first commandment clearly and concisely. Since he is the First and the Only One, since we owe him everything that we are and have, the first fitting response for man is faith in him. To believe in God means to submit oneself completely, mind and will, to God (CCC 143): "You shall worship the Lord your God and him only shall you serve", Jesus replies to Satan (Mt 4:10).

No attitude is better suited to man than this. Nothing makes him so free as serving God. For no one deserves so unconditionally our entire trust; no one is as unshakably the rock and foundation of our hope as he alone is. There is nothing slavish about serving God totally; it is an overflowing of love for the one who first loved us (CCC 2083): "I am the LORD your God, who brought you out of the land of Egypt, out of the house of bondage" (Ex 20:2).

The more we ponder this one truth and allow it to fill our hearts: the fact that God IS, the more our whole life will have direction, meaning, and stability (CCC 222–227). The more we are seized by the fact that God IS, the stronger our love for HIM will become, transforming our entire way of thinking and acting. That is why every deed of the good man is first of all an acknowledgment of God, why every deed of the wicked man is an offense against God's holiness: "I am the LORD."

Faith, hope, and charity are the only appropriate responses to the God who reveals himself to us (CCC 2086). How surely our sense of the good that we must do and the evil that we must stop doing would grow and mature if we would seek first this one and only necessary thing: God himself! How we would realize then that keeping the Ten Commandments means nothing else than loving God with an attentive, ardent heart.

# 31

# Religion is not a private matter

The first commandment obliges us to render to God the worship that is due to him. The attitude or virtue having as its object the worship of God is called in Latin *religio*. *Religio* is manifested in interior and exterior acts of worship, which testify to our dependence on God, enliven our relationship with him, and express our gratitude to him.

The fundamental attitude of *religio* is *devotio*, dedicating oneself to God. This attitude acknowledges our own nothingness, which has received everything from God (CCC 2097).

Prayer is the spontaneous or deliberate expression of our worship of God. It is the milieu in which devotion to God can unfold. Without prayer, the *religio* in man dies and the relationship to God turns pale.

Sacrifice, too, is an expression of *religio*, a sign of devotion, whereby the outward sacrifice must correspond to the inward disposition if the sacrifice is to be genuine (CCC 2100).

*Religio* and the forms in which it is expressed involve the entire man, body and soul; it is not a private matter, because we are social beings. Our Yes or No to God has public consequences, even when we are praying "in secret" in our room.

The twentieth century demonstrated what consequences personal atheism can have when it becomes the official state ideology (CCC 2123). Then it is not long before religion is not even tolerated as a private matter, and a hidden act of worshipping God can become a political crime. This, however, reveals even more clearly the fact that even the most personal fulfillment of a religious duty has public significance. Religion is personal but not private, because it always presses on toward visible actions performed in common, seeks to express itself socially and to have a visible influence on community life.

Do society and the state as such have an obligation to practice *religio*? Do they owe God gratitude and worship? In our pluralistic societies the idea of a state religion is largely outmoded. Must the state then be completely neutral with regard to religion? An atheistic state is surely a contradiction in itself, a "non-entity". The state cannot have the destruction of religion as its goal. It destroys with it—as almost eighty years of Soviet communism demonstrated—the foundation of a flourishing community life. Must the state use the means at its disposal to try to bring about the acceptance of the true religion, the Christian faith? This view, which for a long time was the prevailing view, has clearly been dismissed by the [Second Vatican] Council. After much entirely understandable delay, the Church has developed and set forth her view of religious freedom.

Within "due limits" (CCC 2109; *DH* 7 § 3) the state must respect and safeguard the freedom of individuals, but also of associations, to live and to act in accordance with their conscience, especially in religious matters, and therefore also to proselytize without using coercion or pressure.

The sects worldwide raise the question today of how far religious freedom can go without being detrimental to the common good. Which associations deserve to be called churches and religions and to be officially recognized as such? The very question goes to show clearly that religion is not a private matter. Without *religio*, no commonwealth can thrive.

# 32

# *You shall not make for yourself an image*

The first commandment, it would seem, forbids any kind of image: not only of God himself, who is "'the inexpressible, the incomprehensible, the invisible, the ungraspable'. . ." (*Liturgy of Saint John Chrysostom*, Anaphora, quoted in CCC 42), but also of every sort of living thing "that is in heaven above, or that is in the earth beneath, or that is in the water under the earth" (Ex 20:4). Did the Church somehow "get around" this clear prohibition, inasmuch as she does not only tolerate images but recommends and venerates them? This accusation is made against her over and over again, from the Iconoclasts of the eighth and ninth centuries down to many Reformers of the sixteenth century, especially Calvin. Many (like Martin Luther) permit religious images for purposes of instruction but reject the veneration of them in the liturgy or in private devotion.

The Church did not repeal the first commandment; she simply would not have the authority to do so. Rather, she has interpreted it in the light of the New Testament and the faith experience of the centuries. The meaning of the first commandment is the positive declaration: "I am the LORD your God, who brought you out of the land of Egypt" (Ex 20:2). Because God alone is God, "You shall have no other gods before me" (Ex 20:3). The prohibition of images is the defending wall against idols. Nothing that we produce ourselves, images of deities, images of men, human accomplishments, may become for us an idol, a substitute for God. The prohibition of images is a prohibition of idols, forbidding us to make ourselves slaves to self-made images and artifacts. This prohibition is in force; it is no less valid in our idolatrous age.

What happens, though, when God himself sends us images that we, consequently, have not invented but have received? "God forbids Israel to make for itself images of him, because the people that he has chosen for himself is 'predestined to be conformed to the image of his Son' (Rom 8:29). God forbids man to set up the gangplank of idolatrous images, because he wants to build between himself and man the bridge of the Incarnation. The true image of God will be God himself, who becomes man in order to glorify all humanity" (D. Barthélemy, *Gott mit seinem Ebenbild* [God and his image] [Einsiedeln, 1966], 129).

Because it is God who has given us the gift of an image of himself, his Son Jesus Christ, who is "the image of the invisible God" (Col 1:15), we are allowed to make copies of this image. From very early on, images of Christ were created. The fact that they are also venerated has nothing to do with idolatry, with serving pagan deities. It is not the material that is worshipped but rather Christ whose image is being venerated (CCC 2132). When a mother points to an image of Mary and tells her child, "That is Mary", she does not confuse the picture and the person represented. What matters to her is the reverence and love of the faithful; the image is only a "window", a glimpse of Christ and his saints (from whom he is inseparable). We human beings of flesh and blood need these windows, so that Christ, Mary, and the saints can shine through them into our daily life.

# 33

# God's Name is holy

The name stands for the person. He who gives someone a bad name also strikes at the person himself. He who honors the name honors the bearer of the name. Streets, plazas, and buildings receive the names of persons, who are supposed to be honored thereby.

The second commandment tells us to honor God's Name, to revere it. It forbids the misuse of it in any form. In a wider sense the second commandment concerns reverence for everything that is sacred (CCC 2142).

God has revealed his Name, which means that he has communicated himself, that which is most intrinsically his own. "God has a name; he is not an anonymous force. To disclose one's name is to make oneself known to others; in a way it is to hand oneself over by becoming accessible, capable of being known more intimately and addressed personally" (CCC 203).

We see in the New Testament the full extent to which the revelation of the Name brings about fellowship with God. Jesus considers it his mission to make the Name of his Father known to us, to make us acquainted with him: "I have manifested your name to the men whom you gave me out of the world" (Jn 17:6). Even more: Jesus reveals "that he himself bears the divine name" (CCC 211). So we revere the Name of Jesus, too, as a divine name. How could Paul say that every knee in heaven, on earth, and under the earth must bend at the

Name of Jesus (Phil 2:10; cf. Is 45:23), if this were only a human name?

"Out of respect for the holiness of God, the people of Israel do not pronounce his name" (CCC 209). We could learn a lot from this holy fear and take God's Name less casually in conversation. Many are too quick to pronounce the Name of God, often on occasions that are entirely inappropriate (CCC 2155).

On the other hand, in the Name of Jesus God's presence has touched us so deeply that the heart needs to pronounce it. Love for the Name of Jesus has left its mark on the entire history of the Christian faith. In every Hail Mary the Name of Jesus stands in the middle (CCC 2676), likewise in the Jesus Prayer of the Eastern Church (CCC 435). More than sixteen hundred times the Little Flower uses the Name of Jesus, who is her "only love".

How can we account for the fact that precisely this Name is especially reviled? It seems as though Christianity, indeed, Christ himself, evokes downright blasphemy as no other religion does. Maybe the reason for it lies in the incomparable closeness that God has to us men in Jesus Christ. Because Jesus' love touches the human heart so directly, the danger of hardening the heart is that much greater. Perhaps we encounter blasphemy (insulting God) so often today because the love of God, which gives itself without defense in Christ, is just as defenselessly exposed to all sorts of denial. Could much of the blasphemy that we encounter today, much of the scorn for Jesus and everything that is sacred to Christians, actually be a cry for help, an attempt, despite everything, to be able to believe in love, of which many already despair?

Like all the Commandments, this one too is based on the commandment of love of God and love of neighbor. We revere the Name of Jesus, not out of anxious fear, but out of love. In him we find consolation and deep joy.

# 34

# *You shall keep holy the Lord's day*

Is the third commandment (the sabbath commandment) still valid for Christians? As with the prohibition of images in the Old Covenant, a similar question arises here, whether the seventh day, the sabbath, has not become "outmoded" in the new order of salvation. Christ rose "on the first day of the week", which Christians celebrate as the day of the Lord (*dies dominica*, hence *domenica* in Italian, *domingo* in Spanish, *dimanche* in French) or as Sunday (CCC 2174); can we simply transfer to this first day, though, the prescriptions of the Old Covenant concerning the seventh day?

Let us look first, as the *Catechism* does, at the sabbath commandment. The sabbath is intended, first of all, to call attention to the fact that the entire work of creation is ordered to God (CCC 347). The world is not an end unto itself; it finds its meaning in God's sabbath. Our lives are made for God; in him alone do our hearts find rest (CCC 30). The strict commandment to keep holy the sabbath is not primarily or simply an exterior precept (as it is often misunderstood to be); it helps us, rather, to escape the slavery of work and the idolatry of money. If even God himself rested and "was refreshed" (Ex 31:17) on the seventh day, then man too should cease from work and allow others, above all the slaves and foreigners, to "be refreshed" (Ex 23:12; see CCC 2172). The sabbath reminds us that man is not merely a beast of burden that needs to stop for breath once in a while, but that he is created for God and for eternal happiness with him, of which he already receives a foretaste in the liturgy and in the sabbath rest (CCC 347).

All this is true of Sunday as well, even though the many detailed precepts of the Old Testament are no longer valid for Christians. Sunday even brings the deepest significance of the sabbath to light: that this world is to be perfected in the new creation, which has begun irrevocably with Christ's Resurrection and is already present in the celebration of the Eucharist (CCC 2175).

It is becoming more and more necessary today for Christians to make a very deliberate effort to observe Sundays, not only among themselves, but also in public life. This begins with our choice of words: We should not wish each other "a nice weekend", but rather a good Sunday. We also seem to have forgotten that Sunday is the first day of the week, not the last, even though we experience Monday as the beginning of the week. It is good to begin and to conclude the week with the day of the Lord.

To cultivate the observance of Sunday means, nowadays, to fight against many trends: the fragmentation of family life, the tendency in the working world to work on Sunday, the Sunday "unrest" of hectic travel, and so on.

The communal celebration on Sunday is a great help in giving form and meaning to Sunday (CCC 2181). The celebration of the Eucharist in common on Sunday morning with as many as possible participating is desirable. It should be for all of us a deeply felt need and not just an external obligation to meet the risen Lord in the

Eucharist, but also our neighbor, especially the elderly, the sick, and the children, who need our time and our love. It is for their sake in particular that a Sunday off gives us quality time.

# 35

# Honor your father and your mother

With the fourth commandment, the second table of the Decalogue begins (CCC 2197). It is the first commandment concerning love of neighbor. After God, we should honor our parents in first place. After God, we owe to them our life, our existence. They remind us that we did not create ourselves. We have received our life, and therefore we have no right to dispose freely of our life. Honoring our parents therefore also means acknowledging our status as creatures before God and before one another.

The commandment to honor our parents probably stands at the first place of the second table for another reason as well: someone who honors father and mother will also find the proper measure in the other relationships of human life. He will respect life (fifth commandment), the right order of sexuality (sixth commandment) and of property (seventh commandment); he will use words responsibly (eighth commandment). The fourth commandment thus is fundamental in putting love of neighbor into practice. It is the only commandment to which a promise is attached: "that it may be well with you and that you may live long on the earth" (Eph 6:3; cf. Ex 20:12). The well-being of human society, but also one's personal well-being, depends then on the well-being of this first relationship, which lays the foundation for all other relationships in human life.

The fourth commandment protects the family as the

original cell of human society (CCC 2207). That is why the protection of the family as the Church understands it has such a high priority. Before we treat the subject of the family in more detail, though, two objections should be mentioned.

Why does the fourth commandment speak only about the duty of children with respect to their parents? We are accustomed today to speak about the rights of the child, and if we speak about duties it is about those of the parents first of all. I believe that Sacred Scripture speaks first about the duties of children toward their parents because every human being is a child at first, the child of God and the child of his parents: because being a child, therefore, comes before becoming a parent, and because even parents should never forget that they are children in God's sight and in relation to their parents. This natural order is made still more profound by Christ when he tells us all that we can enter the kingdom of heaven, that is, reach the goal of our lives, only if we "become like children" (Mt 18:3; see also the beautiful book by Heinrich Spaemann, *Orientierung am Kinde* [Being child-oriented] [Einsiedeln: Johannes Verlag, 1989).

The second objection: Did Jesus not himself "relativize" the fourth commandment? "He who loves father or mother more than me is not worthy of me" (Mt 10:37). In another passage he speaks even more radically: "If any one . . . does not hate his own father and mother, . . . he cannot be my disciple" (Lk 14:26). "Hate" here cannot mean "spiteful contempt" but, rather, that the call of Jesus is more important than all family ties. He makes it quite clear: God does not set aside our duties toward our parents (see Mk 7:8–13), but God's call to leave everything behind can also mean to follow Christ in preference to anything else. Jesus himself was obedient to his parents (Lk 2:51), and yet he had to cause them pain by obeying even more the will of his heavenly Father (Lk 2:49).

# 36

# The family

Sociologists rightly point out that "the family" has changed enormously in the course of the centuries. The small modern nuclear family that we know today is not the only form in which the family exists. Three or four generations ago the extended family was still the norm, especially in rural areas: many children (though with a high rate of infant mortality) and at least three generations living together. In ancient times—and even today in parts of Africa that have maintained their traditions—the family was still larger: it embraced the clan, the tribe, that is, the wider network of relatives in which the individual and the immediate family were bound by close ties.

One might conclude from this that the family is "only" one among many possible forms of living together, a changeable form that varies according to the circumstances of the age. The Church, however, champions the conviction that the family is designed by the Creator as the "*original cell of social life*" (CCC 2207). It precedes all other forms of community. It is "prior" to the state and to society (CCC 2202), which is why the public authorities cannot simply exercise control over the family but have a particular duty to protect and promote it. Again and again political utopias have dreamed of abolishing the family, of "liberating" man from "family ties": the children would not be raised by the parents but by a "collective"; everything possible would be done to loosen the marital bond between spouses. Communism consistently proceeded according to this ideology and to a large extent destroyed the family. The consequences for the individual and for society are tragic. In our Western society, too, factors detrimental to the family have left their mark.

Nevertheless there are also signs of serious reflection on the value of the family. What is not learned in the original cell of society, in the family, can be made up only with difficulty through other social units, such as the school, peer groups, or the working world. The call for family-friendly government policies is not a "special interest" of the Church but, rather, springs from a concern for a future worthy of man.

"Where families cannot fulfill their responsibilities, other social bodies have the duty of helping them and of supporting the institution of the family" (CCC 2209). This is especially true for situations, so common today, of "partial families", single parents, mothers in crisis, broken partnerships, dysfunctional families. God's oft-repeated call to his people "to visit orphans and widows in their affliction" (Jas 1:27) is no less valid today. For us Christians, therefore, it has to be an urgent priority to take action in addressing today's forms of family need.

The family is the original pattern of human relations. It is not for nothing that we praise the family atmosphere of a workplace or speak of the "parish family" or view "fraternal" relations among peoples as a desirable goal. The expression "the human family" has meaning only if we all see each other ultimately not just as individuals but as children of the one Father and thus as brothers and sisters (CCC 2212).

# 37

# *Superiors*

"God's fourth commandment also enjoins us to honor all who for our good have received authority in society from God" (CCC 2234). That is a tune we are not used to hearing today. Although honoring not just parents, but all other superiors—the [Austro-Hungarian] emperor first and foremost, and government in general— was once taken for granted, this attitude has changed profoundly as a result of the "cultural revolution" of the sixties and also because of the massive abuse of authority by totalitarian regimes. Any demonstration of respect for government was criticized as "servility", while "authority" in general came to be suspect and was to a large extent demolished.

All this produced much criticism that was justified, but in the process it destroyed much that was good and right. Today it has once again become evident how indispensable the—often ridiculed—"bourgeois virtues" are if the community is to thrive. We realize how valuable it is for a country to have officials who are honest, diligent, eager to serve, incorruptible, just, and faithful, only when these virtues are lost, when corruption, lust for power, self-interest, and arbitrariness gain the upper hand among those who hold authority.

This presupposes, though, on the part of subordinates, that they will show loyalty and a suitable degree of respect toward the authorities: "It is the *duty of citi-*

*zens* to contribute along with the civil authorities to the good of society in a spirit of truth, justice, solidarity, and freedom" (CCC 2239).

All, both superiors and subordinates, must realize that they have a common duty toward something greater, which we can call the "common good" (CCC 1905). This is not an abstraction. It becomes apparent to us in the concrete form that welfare takes in our homeland (another word that is worth rediscovering). Love for one's fatherland demands concerted efforts for domestic peace, for justice, and for flourishing human relations. That is why we owe a debt of gratitude to those who stand up for the common good (CCC 2239).

When politics becomes a dirty word and being a politician is a disgrace, the commonwealth is in danger of falling apart. That is why Christians have always considered it their duty to pray for the secular authorities, " 'that we may lead a quiet and peaceable life, godly and respectful in every way' " (1 Tim 2:2, quoted in CCC 2240).

Nevertheless, obedience, too, has its limits: when something that is unjust, immoral, or contrary to human dignity is commanded, a person is obliged in conscience to refuse obedience (CCC 2242). This is true of parental (CCC 2217) as well as governmental commands: "We must obey God rather than men" (Acts 5:29). This can mean opposing, for instance, nationalistic attempts to make the fatherland an absolute power; intervening to defend the lives of the defenseless where this is no longer guaranteed by the public authorities; to stand up for the right of asylum for the oppressed foreigner where this is denied him, and thus, by solidarity and collaboration, to remind the government of its duties toward the weaker members of the community.

# Church and state

In a certain way the relation between Church and state falls within the scope of the fourth commandment (CCC 2244–2246). For the faithful who make up the Church are also citizens of secular communities, among which the state has a particularly important role to play. Just as every human being belongs to a family and has a father and a mother, ancestors and relatives, so too his affiliation with a state corresponds in a certain way to "the nature of man" (CCC 1882); and just as it is a serious loss for a person when his own family is broken, torn apart, or completely ruined, so it is—not exactly, but in a comparable way—a serious loss for the individual, for families, and for human relations when the state is in crisis, when its institutions fail, its foundations crumble, when chaos and corruption, mismanagement, and the abuse of power take the place of a well-ordered political system.

The first task of the Church as a society of believers who live in a state is to cooperate actively in building up and maintaining the commonwealth. The widespread tendency today to make demands upon the state before anything else must not mislead Christians into thinking likewise of their own interests first and demanding the maximum fulfillment of their wishes.

To the fourth commandment of honoring father and mother is attached the promise of long life and well-being in the land [cf. Deut 5:16]. By analogy the promise also applies to those who, as citizens of the state, share in the responsibilities and offer their services. Those who have the privilege, as we do in Austria, of living in a constitutional state, in which public order is maintained and the institutions function, can easily take it all for granted and fail to realize how much "quality of life" is lost when the state sinks into chaos.

In her relations with the state, the Church should not be primarily concerned about privileges; even so, she certainly has a claim to the right to live and work freely as a community based on religion (CCC 2106). This is important for the state also, which, after all, in structuring its institutions and its life cannot simply be "neutral".

"Every institution is inspired, at least implicitly, by a vision of man and his destiny, from which it derives the point of reference for its judgment, its hierarchy of values, its line of conduct" (CCC 2244). What world-view guides major and minor political decisions? "The Church invites political authorities to measure their judgments and decisions against . . . [the] inspired truth about God and man" (CCC 2244). In doing this, the Church does not intend to interfere directly in political life or to claim any political authority; rather, she wants Christians to be the "leaven" in society: "By constantly evangelizing men, the Church works toward enabling them 'to infuse the Christian spirit into the mentality and mores, laws and structures of the communities in which [they] live'" (CCC 2105, quoting *AA* 13 § 1). The Church, in defending the God-given dignity of every human creature, whether unborn or elderly, foreigner or handicapped, is also helping the state to be "human-friendly". In the light of divine revelation the Church also knows, however, that the state, the Church, and the individual can walk the narrow path of justice only if we constantly renew our efforts and prayers to turn away from what is evil, convert our lives to God, and say Yes to what is good (CCC 1889).

# 39

# *You shall not kill!*

One of the most important encyclicals of Pope John Paul II is entitled *Evangelium vitae*. What life is he speaking about? What Good News about life is he proclaiming? What life does Christ promise? What life does the fifth commandment protect?

Jesus promised eternal life, which consists of fellowship with God (CCC, Prologue) and which he, Jesus, came to bestow. To obtain this life, one must be ready to lose one's life (Mk 8:35). We are reminded of the fact that earthly, temporal life is not the ultimate goal and the highest value. It is better to forfeit bodily life than to suffer the loss of one's soul (Mt 10:28).

The martyrs have witnessed to this, all those who for Christ's sake, remaining true to their conscience and resisting lies and injustice, were ready to lose their earthly life so as not to lose their soul (CCC 2473). "Unless a grain of wheat falls into the earth and dies, it remains alone; but if it dies, it bears much fruit. He who loves his life loses it, and he who hates his life in this world will keep it for eternal life" (Jn 12:24–25).

Can human life therefore be disposed of arbitrarily? The fifth commandment expressly places man's entire earthly life, both of the body and of the soul, under God's special protection: " 'God alone is the Lord of life from its beginning until its end: no one can under any circumstance claim for himself the right directly to destroy an innocent human being'" (CDF, instruction, *Donum vitae*, intro. 5, quoted in CCC 2258).

Life is sacred because God, who creates and preserves it, is holy. A society in which the sense of the divine becomes dull quickly loses respect for life as well. In the early Christian "Teaching of the Twelve Apostles" (*Didache*), the originality of Christianity, in contrast to the contempt for life in the surrounding pagan world, is expressed clearly: "*Do not murder*, . . . do not kill a fetus by abortion, or commit infanticide. . . . The way of death is this. . . . It is the way . . . of men that have no heart for the poor, are not concerned about the oppressed, do not know their Maker; of *murderers of children*, destroyers of God's image; of men that turn away from the needy, oppress the afflicted, act as counsels for the rich, are unjust judges of the poor—in a word, of men steeped in sin. Children, may you be preserved from all this!" (*The Didache*, trans. James A. Kleist [New York: Paulist Press, 1948], 2:1–2, 5:1–2).

Today, in an increasingly neo-pagan world, the Holy Father untiringly speaks of the "culture of life", which is threatened by today's "culture of death" but which is also the only thing capable of overcoming the latter. The Pope observes signs of hope for the culture of life everywhere, even though he deplores the fact that "it is often hard to see and recognize these positive signs, perhaps also because they do not receive sufficient attention in the communications media" (*EV*, 26).

The fifth commandment indicates the extreme limit, which may never be transgressed. Understood positively, it commands an absolute respect for the life of man, who is made in the image of God, and this is sacred.

# 40

# Defending life—comprehensively

The fifth commandment places human life in all its phases, in all its dimensions, under God's special protection. It encompasses protection for the life of the body as well as that of the soul.

That is why the *Catechism* discusses "scandal" under the heading of the fifth commandment—as an offense against "respect for the souls of others" (CCC 2284). Leading others to do evil can amount to killing their souls. That is why Jesus, completely in earnest, cried woe to anyone who gives scandal to "one of these little ones who believe in me" (Mt 18:6). Scandal can proceed from personal behavior, but also from laws that promote the scandal or insufficiently protect against it; and from opinion shapers who have a ruinous effect and devastate the "landscape of the soul". Danger to the life of the body is less to be feared than threats to the life of the soul. To a large extent it is no longer customary to speak of "saving your soul" as the ultimate good, yet Jesus' warning remains as valid as ever: It is of little profit to gain the whole world if we suffer the loss of our souls (Mt 16:26).

A comprehensive defense of human life begins, therefore, with reverence for the souls of others. If this reverence dwindles, the sense of respect for bodily life is also dulled. That is why a "culture of life" requires the "cultivation of souls". This, in turn, will be able to thrive only if the life of the soul, the living relationship with God, is flourishing. Reverence for the spiritual and bodily life of others grows in the same proportion as we personally experience in faith God's care for man, when we realize how precious we are in God's sight, what price Christ has paid for our salvation.

"All human beings, from their mothers' womb, belong to God who searches them and knows them, . . . who gazes on them when they are tiny shapeless embryos and already sees in them the adults of tomorrow whose days are numbered and whose vocation is even now written in the 'book of life'" (*EV*, 61; cf. Ps 139:1, 13–16). This is the reason for the clear, unhesitating No to abortion, which, however, must always be accompanied by every possible effort to support mothers in need and parents in financial straits and thus to counteract the temptation to abort.

Euthanasia is to an increasing extent a further area in which human life is being threatened. Whereas in highly specialized and high-tech clinics there is the danger of therapy at any price (CCC 2278), there are an increasing number of voices (and corresponding patterns of behavior) declaring that the lives of the handicapped, infirm, and incurably ill people are "lives not worth living" and demanding permission to kill these people. Attempts to make suicide commonplace, indeed to glorify it, are likewise part and parcel of this culture of death (CCC 2282). But even today's widespread cult of the body (CCC 2289) supports in principle a culture that is hostile to life. If only the strong, healthy, sexually attractive body has any worth, then consciously or unconsciously this promotes an attitude of "selectivity" that leaves no room for the weak and the sick, the handicapped and the dependent. A comprehensive defense of life is animated by the awareness that every human life without exception is precious in God's eyes and is included under his protection.

# 41

# *Death penalty?*

Hardly any question has stirred up so many emotions since the appearance of the *Catechism* as the question of the death penalty. Does the fifth commandment not forbid killing in principle? But what about self-defense, then? "Someone who defends his life is not guilty of murder even if he is forced to deal his aggressor a lethal blow" (CCC 2264).

Such legitimate defense, when it is a matter of defending one's own family or the common good of the state, "can be not only a right but a grave duty . . ." (CCC 2265). This can mean even "*legitimate defense by military force . . .*" (CCC 2309).

Can the defense of the common good, too, go so far as to require—so to speak "in self-defense"—the institution of the death penalty? That is what the *Catechism* says: In cases of extreme gravity the death penalty is not to be ruled out (CCC 2267). Of course, it immediately restricts this statement to a great extent: Whenever "non-lethal means" are sufficient to defend people from aggressors, the public authority should limit itself to such means (CCC 2267).

When it was being debated whether to reintroduce the death penalty in the State of New York so as to combat crime, the archbishop of New York, Cardinal O'Connor, argued on the basis of this paragraph from the *Catechism* to declare his opposition to the death penalty. Its use is not necessary to protect people against aggressors. In the encyclical *Evangelium vitae* the Holy Father goes one step further: "Today however, as a result of steady improvements in the organization of the penal system, such cases [which would justify the death penalty] are very rare, if not practically nonexistent" (*EV* 56).

This observation is reinforced by the fact that the Holy Father in two passages of the encyclical notes with approval the trend toward the total abolition of the death penalty: "On this matter there is a growing tendency, both in the Church and in civil society, to demand that it be applied in a very limited way or even that it be abolished completely" (*EV* 56).

In *Evangelium vitae*, no. 27, the Holy Father mentions as well, among the "signs of hope" for a growing "culture of life", "a growing public opposition to the death penalty, even when such a penalty is seen as a kind of 'legitimate defense' on the part of society. Modern society in fact has the means of effectively suppressing crime by rendering criminals harmless without definitively denying them the chance to reform."

Is that a final No to the death penalty? In the Latin edition of the *Catechism*, which was published on September 8, 1997, and represents the definitive version, the remarks of the Pope are interpolated. In practice, again and again, the Pope speaks out decisively against the application of the death penalty and asks pardon for the one sentenced to death. The Church knows that crimes will take place as long as the evil of responding violently to violence persists and love of neighbor, indeed, love of enemy is not fully realized. In the light of the Gospel the Church will continue in practice, with ever greater clarity and determination, to proclaim love for one's enemies, as Jesus did, and to say No to the death penalty.

# 42

# War and peace

The fifth commandment protects human life from deadly force. It challenges us, therefore, to combat the root causes of murder and killing. The human heart is the source of all evil thoughts, which then lead to evil deeds (Mk 7:14–23). That is why Jesus declares peacemakers blessed (Mt 5:9). In order to make peace, I must first have found it myself. That, of course, requires a difficult struggle with my own thoughts and passions.

Jesus does not only remind us of the fifth commandment, he also makes it considerably stricter. Even being angry with one's own brother or neighbor makes one liable to God's judgment (Mt 5:22). Overcoming the spontaneous movements of the heart and of the passions in this way is not possible unless assisted by the grace of Christ, who, in his body, brought "the hostility to an end" (Eph 2:16). Whether we have reached this point is evident in our love of our enemy. To love one's enemies as Jesus commands (Mt 5:44–45) is possible only for someone who has conquered revenge and hatred in his heart. Who of us, though, can declare with certainty that he has already found peace in this deep sense and is secure in the possession of it? Therefore it is a question of fighting for it with the help of grace: "Depart from evil, and do good; seek peace, and pursue it" (Ps 34:14).

Peace in society and within a nation, between groups and peoples, is ultimately rooted in the hearts of men. Yet it also requires external conditions: "Peace cannot be attained on earth without safeguarding the goods of persons, free communication among men, respect for the dignity of persons and peoples, and the assiduous practice of fraternity" (CCC 2304). What a blessing it is to be permitted to live in an era of peace is often realized only when peace is threatened or lost. That is why the Church prays so much for peace.

War is not "the father of all things", as they always used to say. The sorrowful experience of human history goes to show, on the contrary, that it is one of the worst afflictions, "[b]ecause of the evils and injustices that accompany all war . . ." (CCC 2307); " 'From famine, pestilence, and war, O Lord, deliver us' " (CCC 2327). To that extent there can never be a "just war". There are, however, to be sure, situations in which defense by military force is morally legitimate (CCC 2309). In view of the enormous destructive power of modern weapons, the conditions for a morally legitimate recourse to arms are to be evaluated with special care.

War does not repeal the moral law (CCC 2312). Even in war, despite the armed conflict, moral principles remain valid. In the Geneva Convention most nations pledged to limit the destruction of war as much as possible and to protect civilians, wounded combatants, and prisoners (CCC 2313).

The effective way to combat the danger of war is to work for justice among men, groups, and peoples. Since we do not yet live in paradise, though, we will always need to be vigilant, too, in dealing with threats to peace.

This means a suitable national defense as well as a prudent policy for [domestic] security and a just and peaceful social order.

# 43

# The sixth commandment

It is the sixth, not the first commandment. Sometimes you get the impression that it has first place, so much is said about it. Often the reproach is heard that the Church has overemphasized it, as if everything revolved around this commandment alone. This overemphasis once existed, there is no denying that. Today, in contrast, we find that it has become the lead story in the media and among the general public, played up and exploited at every turn. What is the original intent of the sixth commandment? "You shall not commit adultery" (Ex 20:14). The commandments on the second table (CCC 2067) are aimed at the milieu of the human family. The subsequent commandments "are concerned with particular respect for life, marriage, earthly goods, and speech" (CCC 2198).

The sixth commandment protects, above all, conjugal love. In the biblical view, human sexuality "is ordered to the conjugal love of man and woman" (CCC 2360). This fundamental conviction also informs the wider, more comprehensive view of the sixth commandment, inasmuch as it also concerns the right way for the unmarried, persons living alone, and adolescents to deal with sexuality.

Unlike many myths, the Bible sees human sexuality as a reality willed by God. It is not a catastrophe, nor is it an accident. The fact that God created man as male and female means that the sexual character of men and women is willed by God and hence has a positive meaning. That is why the Bible has included among its books the incomparably beautiful song in praise of human love between man and woman, the Song of Songs (CCC 1611). Love, as the Song of Songs describes it, in all its brilliant colors and with all the joys of passionate love, is always longed for and sought; it is and remains even today the picture of what lovers hope for.

The Bible also tells, however, about the profound disturbance between the sexes that has prevailed since the original sin, in which man turned away from God and made himself the goal (CCC 398). Since then the inner harmony of man has been upset: body and soul often contend with one another, the passions are no longer subordinate to the reason and the will, and the relations between the sexes are subject to tensions and conflicts (CCC 400). Since then we men struggle to keep the powers of sexuality, which the Creator has placed within us, from becoming ends in themselves and instead to make sure that they are "humanized", ordered and integrated (CCC 2337). The sixth commandment therefore is not primarily a series of prohibitions but, rather, a guidepost to successful dealings with sexuality and learning how to love. Tradition calls this the virtue of chastity or of self-control.

The *Catechism* emphasizes that this is "a *long and exacting work*", that "[o]ne can never consider it acquired once and for all" (CCC 2342), and also that such self-mastery is accomplished " 'by stages of growth' " (*FC* 34, quoted in CCC 2343). And this is not just a matter of personal effort; "it also involves a *cultural effort*" (CCC 2344) to create a climate of respect and reverence for the dignity of the person and for his ability to love.

# 44

# *Open to life*

The sixth commandment protects marriage. That it also, in the broader sense, has to do with the entire order of human sexuality is connected with the fact that, according to biblical and Christian convictions, "[s]exuality is ordered to the conjugal love of man and woman" (CCC 2360). There is scarcely any point of Christian morals that meets with such a massive amount of criticism and such widespread lack of understanding as this one.

Is not, we are asked, the framework of marriage less important than the fact that two people really love each other, whatever their situation may be, married or not, of the opposite or the same sex? And is not marriage often just an occasion for all sorts of unloving activity? The "sexual revolution" of the sixties made possible a far-reaching separation of sexuality and fertility and, with that, a world-view in which the individual's free self-determination, without any restriction based in nature, became the ideal.

This sort of wishful thinking about a life-style that sets its own standards and norms finds itself, of course, more and more often in crisis. The first shock came as a result of the oil crisis. Many became aware that there are limits of growth to our economy and our prosperity, even though the thought of it is repeatedly suppressed. A further shock was and still is the environmental crisis. Our way of life is permanently destroying the foundations for the life of future generations. A more natural way of dealing with the environment is felt by many to be a necessity. Many fear the uncontrollable consequences of genetic manipulation, for instance.

But what does "natural" mean? What notion of nature should be our guide? And is not "culture", that is, cultivating and giving form to nature, a component of mankind? An environment left entirely to itself would not be a place where people could live. The task of cultivating the earth and shaping it was entrusted to man just as was the task of transmitting life: "Be fruitful and multiply, and fill the earth and subdue it; and have dominion over . . . every living thing" (Gen 1:28). That implies, though, man's responsibility both in transmitting life and in subduing the earth. What is the standard for this responsibility? The biblical view is that it consists of collaboration and hence of joint responsibility with God the Creator. The [Second Vatican] Council says on this subject: "'Married couples should regard it as their proper mission to transmit human life and to educate their children; they should realize that they are thereby *cooperating with* the love of *God the Creator* and are, in a certain sense, its interpreters'" (GS 50 § 2, quoted in CCC 2367).

Ever since the encyclical of Pope Paul VI *Humanae vitae*, the question of responsible parenthood has been the subject of an ongoing debate. I see *Humanae vitae* as being something like a prophetic cry. In the year 1968, which was a turning point, the Pope, in an extremely difficult decision reached only after long study of this matter of conscience, said No to the Pill (to put it simply) and Yes to life. At that time only a few people had any idea of how far the attempts to manipulate the transmission of life would go. I believe that Paul VI at that time, more than thirty years ago, wanted to say: Beware! Life is sacred, it is entrusted to us, it is not to be treated arbitrarily.

To walk "natural" paths means to be open to those things in life that are not at our disposal, which we have received, for handing them on is the most beautiful collaboration possible with God's work of creation.

# 45

# The seventh commandment

"You shall not steal", says the seventh commandment. It forbids "unjustly taking or keeping the goods of one's neighbor and wronging him in any way with respect to his goods" (CCC 2401).

But is there such a thing as "rightful property"? Marxism and its practical realization, communism, called into question the very foundations of the right to "private property"—indeed, they radically disputed this right. Accordingly, almost all private property was "collectivized", expropriated and transferred to communal ownership. The practical consequence of this ideology, of course, was that since everything belongs to everybody, everyone tries to help himself to it. In a "deficit economy" such as communism produced, theft becomes a necessity of life and a survival skill. This did lasting damage to the people's moral sense.

At the other end of the spectrum there is the system of *laissez-faire* capitalism, which makes private property an absolute and tries to disengage it from any sort of social obligation. Maximizing profits becomes the ultimate criterion, without any regard for the communal character of all goods, both material and intellectual.

Catholic social doctrine, which was developed as a response to the industrial revolution, clearly rejects both positions as erroneous. It emphatically defends, against communism, man's natural right to own property; it also recalls, though, against capitalism, that the ownership of goods does not represent an absolute right but, rather, by its very nature has intrinsic limits. How can both of these points of view be united: the right to private property and the obligation to return these goods to the community?

They spring from a common source: belief in the Creator. He is the source of everything (CCC 2402). "Infinite Thy vast domain," we sing in the hymn "Holy God, We Praise Thy Name". The goods of the earth are destined for all men. Today we have a new awareness of this, thanks to the insight that the whole earth shares one ecological fate. The air and the water, the environment and the ecology are common to all and entrusted to all. Polluting them or destroying them affects everyone. Hence Catholic social doctrine teaches "the *universal destination of* [the earth's] *goods*" (CCC 2403).

The right to private property is not opposed to this. Pope John Paul II says: "But the earth does not yield its fruits without a particular human response to God's gift, that is to say, without work. It is through work that man, using his intelligence and exercising his freedom, succeeds in dominating the earth and making it a fitting home. In this way, he makes part of the earth his own, precisely the part which he has acquired through work; this is the origin of individual property" (*CA* 31). Property that has been acquired helps the individual to meet his basic needs and also to care for his family, for the community, for those in need. Whatever I legitimately possess "belongs to me", yet it has been given to me "in trust". In the presence of God we are not owners, but stewards. Faithful ones, hopefully.

# 46

# Theft

In the "old" catechism, the main subject treated under the heading of the seventh commandment is the prohibition of personal, material theft (for example, in Thomas Aquinas and in the *Catechism of the Council of Trent*). Today we run the risk of limiting our discussion of the seventh commandment almost exclusively to the economic and social "rules of the game" (cf. J. Pieper, *Grundformen sozialer Spielregeln* [Basic forms of social rules], 7th ed. [Munich, 1987]), the so-called "social doctrine" of the Catholic Church (CCC 2419–2442). The two belong together, of course: without personal respect for the goods of others, no commonwealth can thrive. On the other hand, personal behavior always has social consequences as well, just as, conversely, deplorable social conditions make it much more difficult for the individual to behave according to God's Commandments.

"Stealing" means "usurping another's property against the reasonable will of the owner" (CCC 2408). If this is done by force, moreover, then we speak of "robbery". A person in great need who makes use of someone else's property in order to survive does not commit theft. Conversely, it is not sufficient merely to comply with the laws of the state. Many things that are not within the scope of civil law can also be theft. Saint Augustine tells in his *Confessions* of how as a youngster he, together with other youths, just to be mischievous, stripped clean a neighbor's pear tree that stood near his parents' vineyard, needlessly, for the sheer pleasure of doing something that was forbidden. Probably not even a punishable offense under civil law, but only childish high spirits. Nevertheless, in remembering it, Augustine sees this deed as an expression of the wickedness of his heart, in which God's commandment is written; conscience gives testimony to this, "which not even wickedness can extinguish". The Ten Commandments did not come about through some human agreement; rather, they are engraved on the human heart, a fact that Augustine sees confirmed by his experience: "For what thief willingly lets another man steal from him? Not even a rich thief would allow one in need" (*Confessions* 2, 4).

That Augustine, even in his later years, still has pangs of conscience over a childish theft of some pears is an indication of how sensitive the conscience can be in detecting theft. Not giving back borrowed objects, not turning in property that is found, knowingly possessing stolen goods—all that normally "burns" in the alert conscience; and when conscience no longer responds to such things, it is in danger of becoming dull and mute.

Theft can assume many forms: wasting public monies, corruption, forcing up prices, tax evasion, poorly carrying out work that one has contracted to do (CCC 2409).

What is distinctive about all of these violations against the seventh commandment is that they destroy mutual trust among people. They are therefore profoundly unreasonable, even though they often pretend to be "clever". The basis of all common life, of all commercial relations, is trust. This presupposes mutual trustworthiness (CCC

2410). Someone who does not respect the property of another will soon disregard the other's personal dignity as well and will exploit him for his own profit (CCC 2414). As with all the commandments, the seventh, too, is ultimately about protecting the dignity of the human being.

# 47

# Responsibility for creation

The seventh commandment extends also to proper dealings with the environment. If the goods of the earth are entrusted to all men for their common stewardship and common use, then this also involves responsibility toward future generations. "Environmental sins" are "theft" committed against those who will live after us on this earth. By wasting the earth's resources, by long-lasting damage to the ecology, we today are diminishing the quality of life of our descendants. Interventions into the very order of life (biotechnology and genetic manipulation) produce risks whose magnitude is nearly impossible to assess.

"Environmental ethics" derives its standards, however, not only from the idea of responsibility for possible future consequences, but also and above all from respect and reverence for the integrity of creation (CCC 2415). But what sorts of dealings with inanimate and animate nature, with plants and animals, actually do justice to the reality that is theirs? Where does "environmental science" get its standards? Where does the proper use of material, vegetable, and animal creation stop; where does misuse begin?

The sections of the *Catechism* that discuss morality in dealings with animals have been repeatedly and vehemently criticized, especially by groups of animal rights activists (CCC 2416–2418). Often in these critiques the text of the *Catechism* is quoted in a way that completely distorts its meaning, as though, for example, it were forbidden to love animals, or as if the Church taught the permissibility of any and every sort of animal experiments.

The basic message of the *Catechism* is: Reverence for creation! Everything on earth—natural resources, plants, animals—should be considered by man as creation, as a reality willed and loved by God: "For you love all things that exist, and you loathe none of the things which you have made, . . . O Lord who loves the living" (Wis 11:24, 26).

"*Animals* are God's creatures. He surrounds them with his providential care. By their mere existence they bless him and give him glory" (CCC 2416; cf. Mt 6:26; Dan 3:79–81). But animals are not human beings. We should be benevolent toward them, and, yes, we may love them how many lovely examples of friendships with animals there are in the lives of the saints: the cat of Saint Philip Neri, the dog of Saint John Bosco, the lion (yes, this is well attested to!) of Saint Gerasimus. Nevertheless, love has its priorities. "It is not right to take the children's bread and throw it to the dogs", Jesus says (Mk 7:27). It is not right to love one's dog more than one's own children. But it is not right, either, to torment animals or to let them suffer needlessly. Jesus commanded Peter to cast his nets again, which resulted in fish being killed. Still, no decent fisherman will ever mischievously or maliciously allow the fish to suffer. The Bible does not forbid man to use animals for his food (Gen 9:3) and his clothing (Gen 3:21). This, however, does not justify cruel or barbaric treatment of animals, methods of transporting them that are determined solely by profit, or unlimited animal experimentation.

Reverence for all creatures and the knowledge that we human beings, too, are God's creatures—not owners but stewards of his creation—will help us to find the right balance.

# 48

# *Truthfulness*

Every commandment corresponds to a virtue. Every "you shall not . . ." has its basis in a positive attitude. The Commandments are not merely boundary lines setting off what is not permissible; in the first place they address basic attitudes that enable us to do good and to avoid evil spontaneously, so to speak, from an interior impulse and out of good habits.

To the eighth commandment, which forbids "misrepresenting the truth" in relations with others (CCC 2464), corresponds the virtue of truthfulness. It has a fundamental importance for life within a community: " 'Men could not live with one another if there were not mutual confidence that they were being truthful to one another' ", says Saint Thomas Aquinas (*Summa theologiae* II–II, 109, 3 *ad* 1, quoted in CCC 2469).

Lying destroys this confidence and poisons the atmosphere of interpersonal relations. The century that we have just completed graphically illustrates what happens when a totalitarian regime elevates lying to the status of official policy: everyone mistrusts everybody; truth and lies are constantly mingled; the lie serves as a means to gain power; fear and intimidation are the consequences. Communism feared nothing more than the truth, and nothing hastened its downfall more than the courage of individuals who broke off with lying and spoke the truth,

even at the cost of their own lives. Aleksandr Solzhe-
nitsyn, in *The Gulag Archipelago*, his monumental work
about the communist [slave/concentration] camps, re-
stored to the truth its liberating voice.

The virtue of truthfulness is so vitally important to us
because our mind needs truth as its nourishment, so to
speak. Even a child wants to know and asks insistently so
as to understand. Wanting to know how things really are,
wanting to understand who we are and what events
mean—this is for us a basic human need, but also a moral
obligation that demands effort and sacrifice. The good
inclination toward truth has to combat the bad inclination to content oneself with comfortable, thoughtless
prejudices and with a superficial perspective. The delight
we take in the truth, in comprehending, in understanding, but also in honesty in our demeanor and in our
actions, strengthens us in our willingness to fight for the
virtue of truthfulness and to guard "against duplicity,
dissimulation, and hypocrisy" (CCC 2468).

"Virtue lies in the middle", say the old schoolmasters.
Virtue finds the right proportion between too much
and too little. "Truthfulness keeps to the just mean between what ought to be expressed and what ought to be
kept secret" (CCC 2469). Truthfulness does not mean
communicating everything to everyone. There are things
that one is obliged to keep confidential; this is true
absolutely about secrets learned in the sacrament of reconciliation (CCC 2490), but also about professional secrets. What truthfulness commands us to say in everyday
situations and what it commands us to conceal can best
be gauged by *love of neighbor*. It can judge what truthfulness requires in each concrete situation (CCC 2488). It

is the measure of all the virtues. Only through it do our actions become good and truly human. That is why we should "do the truth in charity".

# 49

# *Media ethics*

"Showing respect for the truth and truthfully informing the public are the greatest commandments for the press." This is the first principle stated in the "Journalistic Code" of the German Press Council.

The Roman Pastoral Instruction on the Means of Social Communication from the year 1971, *Communio et progressio*, formulates this principle even more comprehensively: "Every communication must comply with certain essential requirements, and these are sincerity, honesty, and truthfulness" (*CeP* 17).

But how are these greatest commandments of communication to be put into practice? Often in ecclesiastical circles a negative image of the media prevails. There is an old saying, "Lügen wie gedruckt" (to lie as if it were in print), that addresses such negative experiences, which obviously date from before the rise of the modern mass media. The ever more quickly revolving modern media carousel, the ever more obvious tendency to flatten and coarsen, and the trend toward negative reporting—especially about the Catholic Church—are rightly eliciting reactions of utmost concern.

Of course, if one reads the Church's documents on media questions, one is surprised by the overall positive tone: With Pope Pius XII, the Church sees these media as "gifts of God" (*CeP* 2) because they further those things that are essential to man, indeed, to the Christian concept of God—communion and exchange: "Social communications tend to multiply contacts within society and to deepen social consciousness. . . . The means of social communication can contribute a great deal to human unity" (*CeP* 8–9). Our world is becoming, more and more, one great network of communication: the media gather people worldwide, "so to speak, at a great round table" (*CeP* 19). "The means of communication, then, provide some of the most effective methods of cultivating that charity among men which is at once the cause and the expression of fellowship" (*CeP* 12). Is that too "rosy", too optimistic, a picture?

All over the world the Church is involved in collaborating with the secular media and in reaching people with Church-run media. It is all the more important, then, to be consciously critical of the media, to see the new dangers that loom over us as a result of the media revolution, so as to meet them without anxiety: the danger of "seeking a mass audience" (*CeP* 21); the danger of too much passivity among consumers (CCC 2496); the hazards of the hectic pace of the media routine, which often exposes media producers to great dangers and difficulties; too little time for serious pursuit of the truth, the reduction of complex truth to slogans and "sound-bites"; catering to a "harried and hurried public" that must be attracted by the most striking presentation possible and drawn away from the offerings of competitors (*CeP* 36–40).

Therefore the Church warns that we "should have a clear conception of the predicament of those who purvey information. [We] should not look for a superhuman perfection in the communicators" (*CeP* 41). Of course, in spite of all difficulties, the media, too, must abide by those ethical principles that form the basis of "the Christian conception of how men should live together" (*CeP* 6): respect for human dignity, concern for the common good (CCC 2498), protection from manipulation and the abuse of power (CCC 2499).

The media are a mirror of society. Often they are a distorting mirror or give a one-sided picture. We can also use them self-critically, though, like a preprinted aid to an examination of conscience, which—not always pleasantly—shows us our faults. And we can be happy when occasionally—thank God, it does happen—something of the beauty of the Church, too, is reflected in the media.

# 50

# Art, the true and the beautiful

The true, the good, and the beautiful, says classical philosophy, are so closely bound up with each other that
they are mutually interchangeable. These three together
constitute, so to speak, the fundamental determinants of
being. Everything that is and has existence carries within
itself its goodness, its truth, and its own beauty. This
conviction stood for a long time unchallenged. Even the
"purpose clause" of the Austrian Education Act mentions the true, the good, and the beautiful as the highest
goal of education. This has completely changed. The
"critical" generation likes to ridicule these three goals
and relegates them to a bygone era, of course without
really being able to put anything else in their place. The
mere denial of the status quo, the constant breaking of
"taboos", the unmasking of what has been handed
down—all that cannot continue in the long run to be
the content of art.

The *Catechism* addresses the subject of "art" in connection with the eighth commandment. Art has something to do with the splendor of truth (CCC 2500). Is
that not too uncritical a notion of art? Does art not deal
with truth precisely in the sense that it exposes truth
mercilessly, even its unattractive, painful sides? Is not one
of art's components the sense of suffering, of misery, the
drama of evil and of guilt? Are there not great works of
Christian art, too, that present a truthful view of the

abyss of human wickedness? The tortured, flayed Christ of Matthias Grünewald on the Isenheim Altar has nothing left of beauty; all that remains of him is suffering and death's agony, which we sinners have inflicted on him. And yet this picture not only is disturbingly realistic, but it also has a profound beauty.

Hope shines from within it. John the Baptist points to the Crucified: "Behold the Lamb of God, who takes away the sin of the world." Those sick with the plague, in whose hospital ward the picture of the Crucifixion once hung, could look up to a Christ who had become just like them in suffering. For all its frightfulness, this picture is radiant with the goodness of the Redeemer, the truth of his suffering, and the beauty of hope.

Art, therefore, does not deal only with what is externally beautiful and harmonious, although this is rightly considered to be its primary end (CCC 2501). Gertrud von le Fort, one of the greatest Catholic authors of our [just-completed] century, says of writing (and similar things can be said also of the other arts) that it shares with the Christian faith the "irresistible inclination to embrace the ostracized and the condemned, even the guilty who are condemned, to accompany on their confused path to the abyss those who have gone astray, to draw the failing and the dying to its heart. . . . Genuine poetry remains, unflinchingly, the great lover of the guilty and the lost."

Perhaps the words of this author will help us to understand better some of the ways of contemporary art and to see more clearly where today's artists, in their often bewildering quests, are on the trail of the Savior's truth.

# 51

# You shall not covet

The last two Commandments of the Decalogue ("You shall not covet your neighbor's wife", "You shall not covet your neighbor's goods") are not concerned with evil deeds, the sins of commission mentioned in the sixth and seventh commandments but, rather, with the disposition of the heart from which evil deeds arise: "For out of the heart come evil thoughts, murder, adultery, fornication, theft, false witness, slander" (Mt 15:19). The two final commandments, therefore, are concerned in a special way with the first commandment to love God with all your heart and all your strength. For a heart entirely devoted to God brings forth good fruits; all its desires are directed to what God wills.

The ninth and tenth commandments are in a special way close to Jesus' Sermon on the Mount as well; Jesus, after all, referred to the inmost dispositions of the heart that, long before an evil deed is done, can turn into a sin within a man: "Every one who looks at a woman lustfully has already committed adultery with her in his heart" (Mt 5:28).

"Concupiscence", or the faculty of desiring, is, in and of itself, something good. Together with the spiritual faculties (understanding and will) it is part of the basic equipment of a human being. According to the classical doctrine about man, there are two basic movements in man's "appetitive faculty", or emotions: the "concupiscible" and the "irascible" passions, the power that strives for something and the power that wards something off. Both are necessary for a good, morally ordered life. Since the onset of sin ("original sin"), however, these primordial powers of man have been disorderly; they strive against the spiritual powers, and it takes much effort and a long battle to order them in such a way that they serve the purpose of human life and do not become forces of disorder, indeed, of destruction. Saint Paul often refers to this battle when he speaks of the rebellion of the "flesh" against the "spirit" (CCC 2515): "Walk by the Spirit, and do not gratify the desires of the flesh. For the desires of the flesh are against the Spirit, and the desires of the Spirit are against the flesh; for these are opposed to each other, to prevent you from doing what you would" (Gal 5:16–17; cf. Gal 5:24; Eph 2:3). Concupiscence turns into disorderly desires; the "old man", injured by sin and its consequences, puts up a resistance to this new life that the Holy Spirit wants to foster within us.

This spiritual battle is a part of our daily life (CCC 2516). The heart, of course, yearns for the "fruits of the Spirit": "love, joy, peace, patience, kindness, goodness, faithfulness, gentleness, self-control" (Gal. 5:22–23). These good fruits of a purified heart (CCC 2517) speak for themselves. It may well be that there is no man who does not yearn for them in his inmost being, even though "the works of the flesh" (Gal 5:19) very often have the upper hand in the battle between "spirit" and "flesh". The ninth commandment is an invitation to seek the joy of a "pure heart" (Mt 5:8) and to strive for it.

# 52

# The spirit's yearning

For the third time now we have arrived at the end of a series on the *Catechism of the Catholic Church*. After our discussions on the Creed (published as a book by Dom Verlag in 1994 under the title *Herzstücke unseres Glaubens* [Core concepts of our faith])[1] and on the sacraments (*Quellen unseres Glaubens* [Sources of our faith], 1996, also published by Dom Verlag),[2] this volume, *Wähle das Leben* [Choose life], has been dedicated to the paths of Christian morality.

Where these paths come from and where they lead to is stated already in the first sentence of the *Catechism*: "God [is] infinitely perfect and blessed in himself" (CCC 1). All God's works have no other purpose than this: that his Creation may have a share in his own blessed life (CCC 1; 257). Man, whom he created in his image and likeness (CCC 355), is called by God to decide freely to follow the way that leads to life and to reject the way that leads to destruction (CCC 1696; 1730).

The Ten Commandments are "guideposts to a happy life". Even though most of them are handed down in the form of prohibitions, their purpose in warning us about the paths of ruin is to show us the way of life. The

[1] *Living the Catechism of the Catholic Church*, vol. 1, *The Creed*, trans. David Kipp (San Francisco: Ignatius Press, 1995).

[2] *Living the Catechism of the Catholic Church*, vol. 2, *The Sacraments*, trans. John Saward (San Francisco: Ignatius Press, 2000).

choice between these two ways is made in the heart. "Where your treasure is, there will your heart be also" (Mt 6:21). Where is our treasure? What is to us the most precious thing? What does our heart long for?

"The tenth commandment concerns the intentions of the heart; with the ninth, it summarizes all the precepts of the Law" (CCC 2534). The last two Commandments go beyond sins of commission and turn our attention to the movements of the heart. They challenge us to combat the disorderliness of our desires and to open ourselves to the longings of the spirit.

Greed, avarice, and envy are the principal forms of concupiscence in our fallen state. Greed is an excessive, unreasonable desire for earthly goods (CCC 2536); avarice is an unrestrained desire for earthly possessions and an insatiable craving for more and more of them; envy is sadness, originating in pride, at the sight of another's good fortune (CCC 2539). How do we combat these desires that consume and poison the soul? In the first Beatitude Jesus shows us the way: "Blessed are the poor in spirit" (Mt 5:3). When we stop building our lives upon our own strengths and accomplishments, our own abilities and property, when we realize the poverty of the creature standing before God, then possessions and power lose their attractiveness. We no longer expect consolation and happiness from them. We become poor in spirit in the measure that we rely upon the providence of our Heavenly Father. Anxious care about the future dissolves and gives way to blessed trust in God (CCC 2547).

Such detachment does not come about without a share in the Cross of Christ or without the labor pains of the Holy Spirit, in which the "new man" is formed.

Happy the man who yields to the yearning of the Spirit. Through all the dangers that beset the human heart, He will lead him into the "land of the living", into blessed communion with the living, Triune God.

# Abbreviations

AA   Vatican II, Decree on the Apostolate of Lay People, *Apostolicam actuositatem* (November 18, 1965)

CA   John Paul II, Encyclical, On the Hundredth Anniversary of "Rerum Novarum", *Centesimus annus* (May 1, 1991)

CCC  *Catechism of the Catholic Church*, 2d ed., revised in accordance with the official Latin text (1997)

CDF  Congregation for the Doctrine of the Faith

CeP  Vatican II, Pastoral Instruction on the Means of Social Communication, *Communio et progressio* (January 29, 1971)

CL   John Paul II, Apostolic Exhortation on the Vocation and Mission of the Lay Faithful in the Church and in the World, *Christifideles laici* (December 30, 1988)

DH   Vatican II, Declaration on Religious Freedom, *Dignitatis Humanae* (December 7, 1965)

DV   Vatican II, Dogmatic Constitution on Divine Revelation, *Dei Verbum* (November 18, 1965)

EV   John Paul II, Encyclical, On the Value and Inviolability of Human Life, *Evangelium vitae* (March 25, 1995).

FC   John Paul II, Apostolic Exhortation, The Christian Family in the Modern World, *Familiaris consortio* (November 22, 1981)

GS   Vatican II, Pastoral Constitution on the Church in the Modern World, *Gaudium et spes* (December 7, 1965)

PL   J. P. Migne, ed. *Patrologia Latina* (Paris, 1841–1855)

*PT*   John XXIII, Encyclical, Peace on Earth, *Pacem in terris* (April 11, 1963)

*RP*   John Paul II, Apostolic Exhortation, Reconciliation and Penance, *Reconciliatio et paenitentia* (December 2, 1984)